IN FOCUS

W9-BSL-290

DOMINICAN REPUBLIC

A Guide to the People, Politics and Culture

David Howard

LATIN AMERICA BUREAU

INTERLINK BOOKS
NEW YORK

© 2000 David Howard   All rights reserved.
First published in 2000

In the U.S.:

Interlink Books
An imprint of Interlink Publishing Group, Inc.
99 Seventh Avenue, Brooklyn, New York 11215

Library of Congress Cataloging-in-Publication Data

Howard, David, 1969-
   Dominican Republic in focus: a guide to the people,
   politics and culture / David Howard
      p. cm.
   Includes bibliographical references.
   ISBN: 1-56656-243-0   (paperback)
   1. Dominican Republic - Guidebooks. 2. Dominican Republic -
   Description and travel I. Title
   F1934.5.H69   1999
   917.29304'54--dc21   98-27680
                                                  CIP

In the U.K.:

Latin America Bureau (Research and Action) Ltd,
1 Amwell Street, London EC1R 1UL

The Latin America Bureau is an independent research and publishing
organization. It works to broaden public understanding of issues of
human rights and social and economic justice in Latin America and the
Caribbean.

A CIP catalogue record for this book is available from the British
Library
ISBN: 1 899365 25 7

Editing: James Ferguson
Cover photograph: David Howard
Cover design: Andy Dark
Design: Liz Morrell
Cartography and diagrams: Catherine Pyke, adapted from a map by Kees
Prins and Marius Rieff

Already published in the *In Focus* series:
Argentina, Bolivia, Brazil, Chile, Colombia, Costa Rica, Cuba, Eastern
Caribbean, Ecuador, Guatemala, Jamaica, Mexico, Peru, Venezuela

Printed and bound in Korea

CONTENTS

INTRODUCTION: BEYOND THE BEACHES

For the majority of North American and European visitors, the Dominican Republic is the sunny, holiday-packaged Caribbean isle, the shores of which glisten from the glossy pages of tourist brochures or shimmer across the screens of TV travel shows. The increased popularity of the island as a charter-flight destination during the 1980s helped to resuscitate an economy enslaved by a history of sugar monoculture. Before the advent of mass tourism, the Dominican Republic had hovered at the margins of the regional scene, mostly sidelined from world news since the arrival of Columbus in 1492, save for two military excursions by the U.S. Marine Corps during the twentieth century.

The Dominican Republic, strategically positioned to command the main sea routes between Europe and the American mainland, has historically captured the interest of competing world powers. Initially an important colonial frontier, the island of Hispaniola, which the Dominican Republic now grudgingly shares with Haiti, was the first point of contact between the Spanish *conquistadores* and the Caribbean's ill-fated indigenous populations. In more recent times, the island has been firmly positioned in the North American backyard and frequently forced to play ball to U.S. rules. Viewing it as the first southern line of defense under the Monroe Doctrine, successive U.S. governments have maintained a vigilant and active interest in its domestic affairs. The Dominican Republic remains a symbol of Latin American vulnerability to the colossus of the north.

While lying so long in the shadow of mightier powers, Dominican leaders themselves have more than managed to foment their own share of political and economic crisis. Beyond the beaches and modern tourist resorts lie the remnants of a turbulent history, contemporary society having been shaped in part by the political patrimony of the 32-year dictatorship of Rafael Leónidas Trujillo Molina. Is the yoke of the former dictator finally about to be broken?

The late 1990s marked a sea-change in contemporary Dominican politics. In 1996, Dr Leonel Fernández, the leader of the Dominican Liberation Party (PLD), won the second and deciding round of the presidential elections. The long-running influence of *trujillismo*, most recently personified by the outgoing president, the 90-year-old Joaquín Balaguer, had at last been maneuvered out of power. Or does a political specter remain? Fernández gained victory as the result of a pact with Balaguer's own Social Christian Reform Party, allowing the aging patriarch to remain center stage, albeit veiled from public view.

Fetching water home to the *batey*,
San Pedro de Macorís

Dominican culture juggles a medley of external influences. It is a country with a strong Hispanic heritage, which has traditionally allied itself more with Latin American and European nations than with its Caribbean neighbors. Nevertheless, the Dominican Republic is an important component of the Hispanic Antilles, which make up two-thirds of the Caribbean's population of 35 million. In this sense, the Caribbean is essentially a Spanish-speaking region. The chance visitor to the Caribbean is far more likely to be playing baseball and dancing salsa or merengue, than watching cricket or listening to reggae. Santo Domingo, the Dominican capital with over two million inhabitants, vies with Havana as the largest city in the Caribbean.

Despite its growing reputation as a vacation destination, the Dominican Republic remains little known. Beyond its image as a tourist isle in the sun, the country is associated principally and negatively with political turmoil and economic dependency. Yet there are many other questions worth asking about a country of exceptional natural beauty and remarkable cultural energy. How do Dominicans experience everyday life? What changes and challenges lie ahead for the country at the end of another century of turbulent history? These questions frame the following pages.

1   LAND AND PEOPLE: AN ISLAND DIVIDED

Christopher Columbus arrived on Hispaniola, the second largest island in the Caribbean, on Christmas Day in 1492. Sixteenth-century readers of his journals were tantalized by this land which he "loved best," a tropical isle of fertile soils, verdant highlands and valleys, lush greenery and dazzling coastlines. The indigenous population, he suggested, were distinguished by their kindness, goodwill and gentle nature. The surrounding rivers and mountains promised to bear the gold which adorned the natives in abundance. Columbus, it appeared, had sailed into paradise. He claimed the island for the Spanish monarchs, Ferdinand and Isabella, who had sponsored his expedition, and named it *la isla española* or Hispaniola.

The original Taino inhabitants of the island called their land Quisqueya. Frequently splashed across tourist brochures and now the brand name for a Dominican beer, the word Quisqueya is used today to conjure up pictures of this long-gone tropical idyll. The reality of the encounter between European and indigenous cultures, however, was far more brutal. The island's Indian population was exterminated in little more than two generations after initial contact with the Spanish settlers.

Leaving to return to Spain with news of his discovery, Columbus left 30 men to build a garrison — the first European settlement in the so-called New World. The new inhabitants, however, did not survive to greet the arrival of Columbus on his second visit a year later. The fort was burnt down, the men killed, apparently by indigenous warriors sickened by their greed and violence. During this second journey Columbus moved further east, establishing a settlement of several hundred colonists at what is now the bustling tourist town of Puerto Plata. Moving inland, the Spanish settlers discovered the fertile alluvial soils of the Cibao valley, sandwiched between the mountainous spines of the Cordillera Central which diagonally transect the island.

The new colony was built on coercion. The Spaniards brought with them the *repartimiento* and *encomienda,* systems of procuring local workers through forced tribute from indigenous communities. The rapid decline of this labor source led to the introduction of slaves from West Africa by the first decade of the sixteenth century and the development of the transatlantic slave trade. Santo Domingo became the regional entrepôt for the import of slaves and the export of primary commodities such as sugar, tobacco and coffee. For several decades the island was "the capital of the Indies," the center of Spain's American empire. The importance of the colonial administration faded, however, as Spanish settlers began to by-pass the island and to search for greater riches on the American mainland. The colony declined under the ineffectual control of Spain, and continuing conflicts between French, Spanish and, later, Haitian forces left the colony in social and political confusion until the end of the nineteenth century.

The Dominican Republic finally gained full sovereignty in 1865, after initially declaring independence in 1844. Today the country shares the island of Hispaniola with Haiti, accounting for two-thirds of the island's eastern land mass — an area approximately the size of Ireland. The division of an island territory between two separate states is unique in the Caribbean (except for the tiny island of Saint-Martin/Sint Maarten, which is divided between French and Dutch authorities respectively). This shared insularity has been fraught with a history of antagonism between the two countries.

The societies and economies of the Dominican Republic and Haiti differ quite substantially. The relative poverty of both countries, however, becomes apparent when contrasted against annual U.S. per capita GDP of $22,560. Haiti is economically one of the poorest countries in the world and the most impoverished in the western hemisphere. Average Haitian GDP per head amounts to only $370 compared with the Dominican average of around $1,635. The Dominican Republic has a stronger economy which formerly revolved around the export of traditional agricultural products such as sugar, coffee, cacao and tobacco, but now increasingly relies on tourism, ferro-nickel production and export manufacturing in the so-called free-trade zones. Migrant remittances from abroad provide an additional estimated ten percent of the country's income.

The Cibao

Columbus first landed on the north coast, but after scouring the northern interior in search of gold, he stumbled upon the true wealth of the island — the fertile lands of the center in the region now known as the Cibao. The economic potential of the Vega Real (the Royal Plain) became evident only centuries later. During the eighteenth century, among the rich alluvial plains an incipient merchant class developed from a strong agricultural economy based on coffee and cacao. The wealthy elite of the Cibao came to dominate Dominican politics, providing the country with a long line of presidents and political strongmen known as *caudillos*. As a result of this economic and political pedigree, the Cibao and its capital, Santiago de los Caballeros, have traditionally rivaled the national capital of Santo Domingo, located on the lowland coastal plain to the south.

Santiago, the second city with a population of 700,000, is a busy, grid-patterned urban center for the surrounding agricultural areas. The original settlement was established in 1494 on the banks of the Río Yaque del Norte, but moved to its present location in 1563. With an established merchant elite, and as the traditional hub of the tobacco and rum industries, *santiagueros* have long considered their city to be the true heartland of the Dominican nation.

The smaller cities of La Vega and Moca are important agricultural and administrative centers in the Cibao region. The modern cathedral at La Vega dominates the central square and skyline, while the quieter town of Moca boasts a strong lineage of influential politicians from the wealthy land-owning classes.

Santo Domingo

Despite the claims of Santiago residents, the city of Santo Domingo dominates the country in virtually all aspects, standing out as the political, economic and cultural capital. The city was the site of the first cathedral (1523) and the first university (1538) to be founded in the Americas. The settlement was founded in 1496 by Columbus' brother, Bartolomé, as the site for a new capital. The early colonists had decided to abandon the original settlements on the north coast, which had come under the influence of piracy and fallen into social disarray. Rather than reclaim control of the northern region, the colonial authorities chose to scorch the land, thus reinforcing development to the south.

Santo Domingo became an important base for further Spanish exploration and conquest of the region. Ponce de León sailed from the port to Puerto Rico, Hernándo Cortés set sail for Mexico, and Diego Velásquez left for Cuba from the city. The richness of the city's colonial past spurred UNESCO to designate the historic core a World Cultural Heritage site in 1990 and has since helped to fund the extensive restoration of the many sixteenth-century buildings in the old quarter. The historical importance of the city meant that Santo Domingo took on a prominent role in 1992, especially in the eyes of the government of the time, during the five-hundreth anniversary celebration of Columbus's "discovery of the New World."

A major program of government works, which included the building of a monumental lighthouse near the city center in homage to Columbus, caused bitter controversy. The construction piled millions of dollars onto the country's burgeoning debt burden. The architectural designs were originally conceived by a British engineer in the 1920s, and incorporated plans to finance the monument with contributions from around the Americas and Europe. The funds were not forthcoming, even after a seventy-year

Statue of Columbus in front of the
cathedral, Santo Domingo

Jean-Léo Dugast/PANOS Pictures

wait. Nevertheless, the Dominican government pressed ahead in the early
1990s and began building in the east of the capital. The lighthouse forms
the shape of a recumbent cross with a spotlight that lights up the sky in the
form of a crucifix, power supply permitting. Many low-income residents
were either forcibly removed to accommodate the construction itself or
unceremoniously expelled from nearby neighborhoods in order to "beautify"
the area for visiting dignitaries and tourists. Given the controversial nature
of such extravagant expenditure, hundreds of forcible evictions and the
chronic drain on scarce electricity resources, in 1992 the Pope
diplomatically chose not to attend the inaugural mass, but arrived in the
country a day later.

Controversy surrounds not only the building of the lighthouse but also
its function. The lighthouse was constructed to honor Columbus and to
enshrine his remains which were originally entombed in the capital's
cathedral. Columbus was buried in Spain in 1506, but his body was
exhumed and eventually relocated with that of his son, Diego, to Santo
Domingo during the 1540s. When France took control of the island in
1795, the relics were again moved, this time to the Spanish colony of
Cuba. When Cuba gained independence in 1898, the urn which allegedly
contained the remains of Columbus was to be returned to Spain. In 1877,
however, during alterations to the cathedral in Santo Domingo, a second

urn was discovered which bore the name of Columbus, both inside and out. It is this second find which is now enshrined in the Columbus lighthouse, although the dispute over its authenticity continues between Spanish and Dominican authorities.

Over two million of the total population of 7.6 million now live in the National District. Santo Domingo is a sprawling city, spreading out in all directions from the central colonial zone. The more affluent suburbs to the west dissociate themselves from the popular *barrios* of the northern and eastern zones. A series of busy avenues cut through the city, along which private drivers battle with the chaotic general transport system of dilapidated cars and smoke-belching buses. The Malecón skirts the sea front and provides one of the city's focal points for early-morning joggers and late-night revelers.

Santo Domingo's Colonial Zone: Contested Spaces

The city's old quarter on the west bank of the Ozama River is a fascinating blend of colonial architecture, national monuments, cafés, bars, residential apartments and corner grocery stores. The imposing cathedral and Columbus's palace are the initial lure for most visitors, although much remains hidden around the next corner and embedded in the urban social fabric.

The historic core of all Spanish colonial cities housed the foci of imperial power: the church, the governor's residence, and a town hall or government building are fortified and centered on a main plaza. Santo Domingo, as the first European city in the Americas, set the pattern for other settlements to follow. In 1990, the former colonial zone was established as a World Heritage Site by UNESCO. Renovation work along the Calle Las Damas and Calle Isabel la Católica becomes immediately evident during even a short stroll or cursory glance.

During the colonial period, the city center signified the dominance of the Spanish authorities over the conquered indigenous population and the imported African slaves. Power relations had their architectural expression. All monies, taxes and trade had to pass through the city's port; the rural hinterland remained distant and dependent. Today the city center remains a contested space, the site of numerous business ventures amid the flurry of shoppers, residents, tourists, street hawkers, guides, taxi drivers, and police officers. While café-owners and solicitors vie for the traveler's dollar, informal food vendors fend off subtle police pressure or face direct eviction during government crack-downs to "reclaim" the streets and present a more ordered façade for the visitor. City residents pack the central pedestrian mall of El Conde on weekday evenings and on the weekends. The Parque Independencia, the site of the first declaration of Dominican independence in 1844, is the occasional destination of political rallies or protest marches. While the city's population continues to expand, the sprawl of suburbs to the east and west of Santo Domingo has done little to detract from the capital's historic heart. It remains an active hubbub of shoppers, watchers and walkers alike.

Santo Domingo, the colonial zone   *Jeremy Horner/PANOS Pictures*

Central Highlands

Since the arrival of Columbus, two-thirds of the country's original forest has been felled. An ominous prediction in the early 1970s, which forecast that all the native forest would be destroyed by 1990, spurred the Dominican government toward a policy of active conservation. Most of the remaining forest is located in the temperate highlands of the Cordillera Central, where the vast tracts of pines are protected within the National Parks of Armando Bermúdez and José del Carmen Ramírez. The Sierra Plan, centered on the region around San José de las Matas, is the most recent of several schemes to reforest the country. The Dominican government has also been actively involved in the United Nations Global Environmental Facility program to encourage bio-diversity within its borders.

The highest mountain in the Caribbean, Pico Duarte (10,500 feet), lies at the heart of the central highlands. Dominicans regularly flock to the fresh climate of the upland areas, often referred to as the country's "little Switzerland." In winter, the higher regions receive frosts and, very occasionally, a glimpse of snowfall. Jarabacoa and Constanza, surrounded by the pine forests, are popular hill resorts in the summer. Ecotourism is slowly developing, focusing on the range of scenic trekking routes, swimming holes and waterfalls. The main substance of the region's economy, however, relies on the temperate climate for the cultivation of fruit, vegetables and flowers for export to the U.S.

Crafts and souvenirs at Boca Chica

Julio Etchart/Reportage

The Beach Perimeter

Tourism helped to drag the Dominican economy out of the doldrums during the late 1980s and the early 1990s. UNESCO has described beaches in the Dominican Republic as some of the best in the world: white sands, palm trees and lush vegetation are on offer in abundance. The tourist industry is located in several main resort areas along the northern coast near Puerto Plata, to the east at Punta Cana, and along the southern coast, stretching from Santo Domingo toward La Romana. The peninsula of Samaná in the northeast of the country has been marked out for further development, as has the more remote coast around Barahona in the far southeast. Enclave resorts are often delimited by perimeter fences, with notices offering stern warnings to non-residents who may stray onto hotel property.

Puerto Plata, the main tourist center in the north, forms part of the so-called Amber Coast due to the rich deposits found in the region. The town was founded in 1502, but deliberately abandoned at the end of the century by the Spanish authorities due to high levels of clandestine commerce between local merchants and passing privateers from France or England. After being repopulated in the 1730s by families from the Canary Islands, the town remained relatively quiet until the tourist development of the 1970s. The completion of the Playa Dorada resort complex of fourteen hotels to the east of the old center radically changed the local economy and led the way for tourist development throughout the country as a whole.

Sosúa, fifteen miles east of Puerto Plata, is another coastal resort, but perhaps better known for its Jewish heritage. As part of a resettlement program in the 1940s, 600 Jewish refugees from Eastern Europe were invited to occupy the area. The settlers established themselves and developed a now famous local dairy and meat industry. The site of the original Jewish settlement has been swallowed by the encroaching tourist development, but the tradition remains. Farther along the coast, the windswept waters off Cabarete have gained an international reputation as one of the world's leading locations for windsurfing.

The town of Samaná in the far northeast of the country was founded by families from the Canary Islands in 1756. African-Americans who were invited to settle during the late eighteenth century brought with them the English language and the Protestant Church, both of which survive to some extent in the area today.

On the southern coast, Boca Chica, fifteen miles east of Santo Domingo, is the principal beach resort for the capital. Intensive tourist development changed the nature of the locality beyond recognition during the 1980s. At the weekends, the beach is crowded to capacity with the arrival of the capital's population ready to soak up sun and rum. Juan Dolio, another popular beach with both Dominicans and foreign tourists, lies farther east on the way to La Romana, a large sugar town and the former Dominican headquarters of the all-powerful U.S. Gulf and Western company. Beyond the cane-field rail terminus and the pervasive aroma of sugar, the Casa de Campo offers the affluent visitor the "premier resort complex in the Caribbean" and a mock Italian artists' village at Altos de Chavón. Situated between La Romana and Santo Domingo lies the town of San Pedro de Macorís. What the city lacks in terms of beaches, it more than makes up for with baseball prowess. San Pedro has provided a long list of famous Dominican players who have gone on to find greater fame and fortune in the U.S. major leagues.

Global Pastiche: Renaissance Italy Goes Tropical

Three miles east of the $400-per day Casa de Campo resort, lies another product of its creator, Charles Bluhdorn. One story suggests that as a gift to his daughter, the president of the U.S. multinational, Gulf and Western, constructed a mock Italian Renaissance village, the Altos de Chavón. The replica was to be perfect; finances were no obstacle. Bluhdorn's company owned the most profitable sectors of the sugar industry and most of the nearby town of La Romana. Another version of the events behind the village's creation involves fraudulent company practice, threats of legal action by the Dominican government after breaches of contract

Altos de Chavón

regarding business agreements, and a resulting out-of-court settlement to fund development projects in the Dominican Republic. Two such misguided schemes built in the 1980s were the Casa de Campo and the Altos de Chavón.

The Casa de Campo is a combination of pristine lawns, villa-to-villa golf courses and electric golf carts. Minitas Beach serves a purpose, but the real action takes place on the fairways, at the equestrian center or at the shooting range. The Altos de Chavón, billed as an "international artists' village," is perched high on the cliff tops overlooking the spectacular valley of the River Chavón. Bluhdorn intended his daughter's gift to double as "the living expression of the cultural and historical values of the Dominican people." Both fall short of commonly perceived concepts of popular social development.

Gulf and Western initially invested in Dominican sugar production in 1967, buying the U.S.-owned South Puerto Rico Company, which owned 450 square miles of land around La Romana. The newcomer became the largest private landowner in the Dominican Republic, controlling eight percent of all arable land in the country. During the 1980s, the annual turnover of Gulf and Western surpassed that of the entire country's Gross Domestic Product. Gulf and Western sold its Dominican assets in 1985, but the Altos de Chavón remains as a bizarre sideshow to the luxury tourist enclave of the Casa de Campo. Artists, international with respect to air miles rather than by repute, continue to seek inspiration amid the mock *ambiente italiano*, occasionally bothered by bemused bus groups of tourists sauntering through this Caribbean patch of an imaginary European past.

Several national parks are located on the Dominican coast, most notably Los Haitises, near Samaná, where mangrove swamps, caves and unique *mogote* rock formations have attracted the worldwide attention of ecologists, geologists and tourists alike. The Parque Nacional del Este in the southeast of the country includes La Isla Saona, a small island which boasts pre-Columbian cave paintings and rare fauna, notably the white-headed dove, the rhinoceros iguana and turtles.

Borderlands

The heavily vegetated landscape of the Dominican Republic contrasts starkly with the denuded and barren physical landscape of neighboring Haiti, particularly along the border region. Straddling the border, Lake Enriquillo is an impressive inland lake lying between 13 and 130 feet below sea level. The lake's water is three times saltier than the sea and provides the basis for a varied range of flora and fauna. The Islas Cabritos National Park hosts a large crocodile population and many forms of cacti.

The dry scrub of the frontier zone is marginal land in economic as well as environmental terms, but the borderlands are very much part of the Dominican political focus. Recent government plans to develop three industrial free-trade zones along the border stem partly from the ongoing fear that the territory is being depopulated by Dominicans and coming more under the influence of an expanding Haitian population. The massacre of thousands of Haitian peasants on Dominican border territory in 1937 provides the most vivid and violent example of this "Dominicanization" policy.

On the way to the frontier, west from Santo Domingo, lies San Cristóbal. This small town is the birthplace of the former dictator Rafael Leonidas Trujillo and, ironically, the site for the signing of the first democratic constitution in 1844. The frontier outposts of Pedernales, Jimaní and Dajabón are essentially garrison towns. The Dominican military presence is highly evident along the roads near the border. Regular checkpoints and random spot checks of vehicles give the Dominican side a sense of being under siege from the alleged hordes of Haitians poised to flood into the countryside. During the UN embargo against the Haitian military junta in the early 1990s, the border towns were the focal points for many midnight crossings of restricted commodities and illicit trade.

The Myth of the Indian

The first inhabitants belonged to several ethnic groups, namely the Lucayo, the Cigüayo, the Taino and the Carib, who lived by a combination of hunting, gathering and basic agriculture. Following the Spanish appropriation of the island during the sixteenth century, the imposition of harsh working and living conditions and imported European diseases led to the rapid demise of the indigenous population. A Spanish friar, Bartolomé de las Casas, spoke out in support of these groups, but only to argue for the replacement of indigenous slave labor with African. Africans, argued Las Casas, could never have Christian souls and thus were legitimate objects for enslavement. The slave trade and Spanish colonization shaped the island's demography. Today's inhabitants of the Dominican Republic largely share mixed African and European ancestries.

Most Dominicans argue that race does not really matter in the Dominican Republic. "When the light's switched off, we're all the same color" is a commonly heard phrase. However, many Dominicans would consider it offensive to be labeled as *negro* or even *mulato* as this latter term still retains the often negatively perceived image of black identity, whereas elsewhere in the Caribbean it incorporates a strong element of white identity. Indeed, the external perception of the Dominican Republic is often that of a mulatto nation. Few Dominicans, however, would describe themselves or the population as a whole as mulatto.

Some observers divide the population of the country into various proportions — 65 percent mulatto, 15 percent *blanco* or European and 15 percent black are the usually quoted figures, with the remaining five percent of the population made up of other ethnic groups, such as Chinese or Lebanese. These figures, however, are fairly meaningless, as the varieties of skin color and phenotype do not fall into neat groups. More importantly, what to one person may be *mulato*, will be *negro* to another. Racial terms are by and large highly flexible, and Dominicans describe race with a plethora of color-coded terms, ranging from coffee, chocolate, cinnamon and wheat, to *indio*. The latter term translates as "Indian," a much-used reference to the island's indigenous inhabitants before the arrival of Columbus.

Three main ideas have been suggested for the origin of the term *indio*. It may refer purely to skin color, providing an alternative to *mulato* without the connotation of African origins. It has also been suggested that the concept is derived from Columbus' mistaken belief that he had actually arrived in India. Finally, the use of the term has been linked to the rise of *indigenismo*. In Mexico, *indigenismo* was an important element of post-revolutionary ideology, emphasizing the indigenous element in Mexican national culture, as in Manuel Gamio's *Forjando patria* (1916). "We are Indian, blood and soul," wrote Gamio. "The language and civilization are Spanish." The influence of *indigenismo*, however, was limited in the Dominican Republic, even if attempts were made to resurrect an indigenous heritage toward the end of the nineteenth century. Unlike other Latin American countries, the indigenous population in Hispaniola was virtually nonexistent after fifty years of European colonization.

The concept of *indio* identity was actively worked into popular and official psyches during the era of Trujillo's dictatorship. School text books, the press and political rhetoric propagated the indigenous emphasis to dispel an African heritage and to separate the Dominican Republic from Haiti. To be a Dominican was above all not to be a Haitian, and the idea of a pre-Columbian national identity became an institutionalized myth during the *trujillato*. The legacy remains potent. A recent editorial in a Dominican-American newspaper heralded the importance of "Indianness" as an affirmation of "our identity as a people." Dominican Spanish, it is often argued, has been polished and enriched by many indigenous words. The fervor to produce a verifiable indigenous heritage has led to a number of scientific studies of dubious merit, involving the analysis of blood types, facial features and varying denture patterns.

The faceless ceramic dolls made famous by the artisans of El Higuerito in the Cibao belie the importance of physical features in Dominican society. Race is very much related to visual aesthetics: people have "fine" or "bad" hair, a "clear" or "burnt" complexion. Social prejudice is frequently phrased in color terms, and being "white" remains a social and discriminating ideal for many. In job advertisements which ask for employees of "good presence," there is an implied bias toward a fair complexion. It is still rare for banks to be staffed by dark-skinned cashiers. A recent poll of university students asked if they would marry a darker-skinned partner. Fifty-five percent replied that they would not, frequently expressing their concern for the "corruption" of physical appearance through "race mixing." Popular sayings or folklore often incorporate negative images of darker skin colors.

Race and racism run unusually deep in everyday Dominican society. The reasons for this national obsession are many and varied, but a starting point for understanding the importance of such issues lies in the country's relatively short history and its turbulent relationship with neighboring Haiti.

2   HISTORY AND POLITICS: LIMITS OF DEMOCRACY

Electoral politics have had a controversial history in the Dominican Republic. In the 1960s, after three decades of authoritarian rule under dictator Trujillo, his brutal regime was succeeded by the political guile and manipulation of Dr. Joaquín Balaguer. Balaguer stayed in power for 30 years, until 1996, letting go temporarily due to international pressure, during two terms between 1978 and 1986. His Social Christian Reform Party (PRSC) was forced to accept defeat again in the 1996 presidential elections, which were heralded by some as the first non-fraudulent elections in the country's history.

Civil conflict, U.S. invasion, embittered enmities, fraud and racialized politics have scarred the political landscape of the Dominican Republic for much of the present century. Many believe that the current president, Leonel Fernández, heralds a modern generation of politicians who will usher in a more open form of democracy, as the old political dinosaurs exit the stage. Others would claim that these new actors merely play with the same script, loosely concealed behind younger masks.

Early Dominican History

Following the onset of Spanish colonization, Hispaniola was successively the largest gold then sugar producer of the Caribbean colonies, before becoming the region's most important cattle ranching economy during the seventeenth century. At one point there were 40 head of cattle for every inhabitant. Given the great economic and strategic potential of Hispaniola, the island was highly prized by competing European powers. Francis Drake headed sixteenth-century English interests when his pirate forces sacked Santo Domingo in 1586. During the latter half of the seventeenth century, Hispaniola was invaded by French settlers who slowly began to occupy the western part of the island. This new French settlement was called Saint Domingue. Soon tobacco plantations were established which built profitable trade relations with the less developed eastern part. Under the Treaty of Ryswick in 1697, the western part was formally handed over to France following years of border disputes and tension between the two parts of the island. During the eighteenth century, French Saint Domingue continued to develop an affluent plantation economy, extending its export production to sugar, coffee and cotton. By the 1780s Saint Domingue was the wealthiest colony in the world, "the pearl of the Antilles."

Toussaint L'Ouverture

The Spanish territory also profited from this development, largely through the export of cattle to its neighbor. In the French colony, the number of African slaves increased dramatically as the plantation economy demanded a ceaseless expansion of labor. In 1739, there were 117,000 slaves in Saint Domingue, but as the century drew to a close there were over half a million. By then the slaves formed nearly 90 percent of the total population. Mortality rates were appallingly high, but some slaves managed to escape across the border into the less populated Spanish sector.

The 1789 French revolution heralded a period of tumult for both parts of the island. Two years later, the slaves of Saint Domingue began an insurrection against their white masters which was to last for thirteen years. During that time civil war and inter-European conflict on the island raged almost continuously, resulting in a confusing sequence of events.

In 1795, Spain ceded the eastern part of the island to France under the Treaty of Basle. At that time, revolutionary France was only nominally in control of its own colony, the insurrection having overthrown the old colonial order and produced a new leadership of former slaves who formed an uneasy alliance with commissioners sent from Paris. The same year, Toussaint L'Ouverture, the general-in-chief of the armies of Saint Domingue and a former slave leader, declared the island "one and indivisible." The eastern part of the island was occupied and slavery abolished, only for L'Ouverture's forces to withdraw within two years as a French army landed in the east. L'Ouverture was captured and sent back to France, where he died in prison in 1803. However, his successor, Jean-Jacques Dessalines, defeated the French forces in the west of the island and declared Haiti independent in 1804 — the first independent republic in the western hemisphere with a majority population of African descent. The eastern sector was returned to Spain in 1809 after the French finally gave up their attempt to keep a foothold on the island.

Differences between modern-day Haitian and Dominican societies have their origins in the different colonial regimes which governed each territory.

During the eighteenth century, Saint Domingue was by far France's most important colony, providing half of its transatlantic trade. A booming plantation economy produced sugar for the insatiable European market. The intensity of production meant that hundreds of thousands of Africans were brought to the French colony as slave labor for the plantation system. Many of the wealthier, lighter-skinned population emigrated or were killed as the thirteen-year conflict which created the new Haitian state took its course. The result was to leave a Haitian population with an overwhelming majority of African descent.

The situation was somewhat different in the eastern part of Hispaniola. After initial interest during the sixteenth century, the Spanish colony of Hispaniola was largely ignored by the new colonists, who were more inclined to join the rush for the rumored gold and riches to be found on the mainland of Central and South America. The eastern part of the island, in contrast to the sugar economy of what is now Haiti, had fewer plantations and hence less need for an enslaved workforce. Cattle ranching was important but was much less labor-intensive than sugar production. As a result, far fewer African slaves were imported into the Spanish colony.

Occupation and Independence

Despite several armed Haitian incursions into the eastern part of Hispaniola, the island was not joined under a Haitian government until 1822, when Jean-Pierre Boyer invaded and occupied the Spanish colony. Haitian control signaled the formal end of the Spanish colonial regime of slavery, but it also meant that the Dominican Republic would gain its independence not from a metropolitan colonial power, but from Haiti — a black republic. Many Dominicans claim that the period of Haitian occupation was one of tyranny and backwardness; others point out that Boyer broke the Catholic Church's near monopoly on land and created the conditions for an independent peasantry. Nonetheless, resentment against the Haitian occupation grew, and a nationalist movement began to take shape, especially in the main city of Santo Domingo.

The three "founding fathers" of the republic, Juan Pablo Duarte, Francisco del Rosario Sánchez and Ramón Mella, the *Padres de la Patria*, declared Dominican independence in 1844, taking advantage of political turmoil in Haiti to expel the occupying forces. Duarte was quickly removed by rivals, however, and his brand of nationalism forgotten. Politics in the new state were dominated by competing strongmen who sought to defend the country against renewed Haitian invasion and bolster their own position by actively inviting foreign intervention. Aware that the republic was strategically attractive to the U.S. and European powers, successive leaders

Columbus' own sketch of northern "la española", or northwest Hispaniola

tried to persuade the U.S., France or Britain to impose a protectorate and hence deter Haitian ambitions. Two decades of political strife and violence ensued, resulting in a request for Spanish protection and re-colonization in 1861. In an unprecedented occurrence, Spain agreed to retake control of the independent country. The four years of restored colonial rule were a disaster, however, and Spanish rule finally came to an end with the War of Restoration in 1865, after fierce conflict between Dominican nationalists and Spanish sympathizers.

The 22 years of Haitian occupation and subsequent liberation from Haitian control made a fundamental mark on future Dominican-Haitian relations. Despite increased access to power, it was always more necessary for darker-skinned Dominicans to demonstrate their national and cultural identity as distinct from the Haitian "enemy." Signs of African ancestry among "well-to-do" or "respectable" Dominican families were often blamed on Haitian atrocities during the occupation. A revulsion for all things Haitian legitimized a collective aversion to African ancestry. Consequently, Dominican *mulatos/as*, explicitly rejecting Haiti's cultural identity, aimed to forge an entirely separate Dominican nation of Hispanic and indigenous ancestry.

Late nineteenth-century Dominican history charts the ongoing factionalism and a litany of ephemeral governments. Periods of stability corresponded with autocratic rule, most notably the twelve-year dictatorship of Ulises Heureaux (1887-1899) during which the foreign debt of the country burgeoned to a stifling $32 million. Heureaux was in many respects a prototype for Trujillo. Commonly known as Lilís, he imposed a ruthless tyranny and led a notoriously extravagant lifestyle.

The Rise of Trujillo

Two critical events shaped Dominican society during the first half of the twentieth century — the U.S. occupation between 1916 and 1924 and the rise to power of the dictator Trujillo. The two were closely linked: U.S. President Franklin Roosevelt was reportedly moved to describe Trujillo as "a true son of a bitch, but he's *our* son of a bitch."

Following the assassination of Heureaux, Dominican politics and finances collapsed into chaos. The occupation of the country by U.S. marines stemmed from the mounting debt burden and the reluctant agreement of the Dominican government to place control of the country's customs (and hence ability to repay creditors) under U.S. administration in 1905. Relations with the receiver sent from Washington were never good. Growing fears of political and economic anarchy led the troops to be sent in to protect U.S. interests in May 1916.

Unlike the occupation of Haiti a year earlier, the U.S. landing forces did not face a country undergoing violent upheaval, nor did they have a compliant government to front their political and economic maneuvers. Direct martial law was imposed until a provisional presidency was established in 1922. The U.S. military presence remained until elections were held in 1924. The eight-year occupation created a strong nationalist sentiment based on anti-American feeling. Under marine control, communal lands were broken up and U.S. investors arrived in the country to take stakes in the expanding sugar industry. A guerrilla insurgency pitted landless Dominican peasants against the well-armed U.S. forces.

Nevertheless, the occupation also provided a relatively modern infrastructure of roads, ports and bridges, a well-trained national guard and the apparent basis for orderly politics. Having convinced themselves that the Dominican Republic was safe for U.S. investors and ruled by a friendly government, the marines left. Within a decade Trujillo had shattered the illusion of stability by establishing one of the most ruthless dictatorships in modern Caribbean and Latin American history.

Trujillo consolidated his power base during the late 1920s and 1930s. As a member of the national guard he had gained a series of promotions and worked his way up to commander-in-chief by 1927. Machiavellian instincts and political guile more than made up for his limited formal education. In May 1930, after shrewdly distancing himself from an earlier failed revolution, he was elected president of the republic. By the mid-1930s, the evolution to an authoritarian government via a series of puppet presidents was evident.

US cavalrymen in the Dominican Republic, 1916

Trujillo's control became total. For 32 years, he governed the Dominican Republic as his personal fiefdom. Ten percent of all state employees' salary went to the Dominican Party, the political machine of the regime and the only legal party in the country. By the time of his assassination in 1961, Trujillo and his family controlled 80 percent of the country's industrial production. It has been estimated that 60 percent of all Dominican families depended on Trujillo-owned enterprises. Among the honors and titles which he regularly bestowed upon himself were the Benefactor, the Chief, the Father of the New Homeland and the Restorer of Financial Independence. Santo Domingo was re-named Ciudad Trujillo for good measure in 1936.

Government ideology reinforced the notion of the Dominican Republic as a Hispanic, Catholic and largely white nation. Firstly, Haiti was consistently portrayed as a threat, the antithesis of the renovated national image. Secondly, Trujillo lauded attempts to "save" the Dominican nation from "Africanization" and the illegal entry of Haitian immigrants. African influences were considered non-Dominican and, thus, a subversive challenge to the state.

In the mid-1930s, Trujillo aimed to establish Dominican claims to the border territory by blocking further Haitian residence in the region and

Dictators discuss, Trujillo meets Franco

fostering a stronger sense of Dominican identity. For over a century and a half there had been no mutually recognized border between the Dominican Republic and Haiti. The frontier population consisted of many *rayanos/as*, people of mixed Haitian and Dominican descent. Many Dominicans in the border area spoke Haitian *kreyòl* as their first language, were followers of voodoo and used the Haitian *gourde* as the popular unit of currency. Of great concern to Trujillo was the purported "darkening" of the population as more Haitians migrated to settle in the provinces.

Trujillo feared the growing influence of Haitian culture in Dominican territory. A boundary agreement in 1936 established the basis for a program of Dominicanization. The most brutal illustration of this policy to reclaim the nation came a year later with the massacre of approximately 15,000 Haitians and dark-skinned Dominicans, residents in the border zone. Suspected Haitian workers were challenged by Dominican police and military patrols to pronounce the Spanish word *perejíl*, meaning parsley. The combination of "r" and "j" was thought to be difficult for any Haitian to master, thus providing proof of their nationality and deciding their fate at the hands of the Dominican interrogators. Continuing expulsions of Haitians were carried out by the Dominican military and an intense religious and educational campaign was pursued in the border areas. A select corps of Frontier Cultural Agents disseminated Dominican propaganda, while a network of highways was constructed to reduce the physical and economic isolation from the rest of the country. Houses were constructed in traditional

Dominican styles and agricultural colonies promoted. To "lighten" the population, Trujillo attempted to encourage the resettlement of refugees from Eastern Europe, Italy and Japan in the Dominican borderlands.

Trujillo sought complete dominance of social, political and economic spheres. He maintained power for over three decades either as president in name or via an appointed titular head of state. The loyalty of strategic civilian and military appointees was assured through coercion, bribery and blackmail. Trujillo carried out a large-scale public works program during the early days of his regime, closely attuned to the furtherance of his own vast fortune. Artificially high prices for Dominican products following the Second World War swelled public and private coffers. By 1947 Trujillo was able to pay off the country's external debt by signing a single check for over nine million dollars.

Whereas dictatorships enjoyed seemingly greater tolerance during the 1930s, after the war their tyranny was much less acceptable to the international community. Pressure from the newly-formed Organization of American States (OAS) forced Trujillo to contemplate improving his image overseas. However, this did not dissuade him from contemplating the assassination of critics abroad; at one time this allegedly included the Pope. Internally, media and political censorship remained complete, and indeed arbitrary persecution increased as his fears of dissension grew. Few dared to write or speak out against the regime, and those who did were soon added to the growing list of dead or disappeared.

Death of the Butterflies

The brutal murder of three sisters and their chauffeur from the Cibao has come to typify the savagery of Trujillo's regime. A compelling novel by Julia Alvarez, *In the Time of the Butterflies* (1995), recounts the horrors of the dictatorship and focuses on the tragic lives of the Mirabal sisters. Patria, Minerva and María Teresa Mirabal were the wives of three prominent political activists, imprisoned for their verbal resistance to the *trujillata*. They had left the small market town of Salcedo to travel to Puerto Plata to visit their husbands in jail. On their return to the Cibao during the evening of 25 November 1960, they were ambushed on an isolated mountain road by Trujillo's agents. The shooting was coordinated by the notorious thug, Johnny Abbes, who had been appointed head of the infamous Military Intelligence Service (SIM) in 1957.

The funeral of the Mirabal sisters galvanized the single most significant public protest against the evil of Trujillo's regime. Their deaths and the subsequent international outrage marked the final spate of blood-letting before the blind tolerance of the U.S. government ran out, provoking the Central Intelligence Agency to help the dictator's opponents plot an end to his tyranny. The days of the dictator were numbered. The OAS had condemned outright Trujillo's attempted assassination of the Venezuelan President, Rómulo Betancourt, only a few months before. Growing popular resentment, and the clandestine support of the U.S. authorities, spurred Trujillo's enemies to act. On the evening of May 30, 1961, the dictator was surrounded and gunned down whilst traveling by car from the capital to San Cristóbal to visit one of his numerous mistresses. His assassination heralded the end of an era of brutality and repression, but violence and injustice remained an all too evident part of Dominican politics during the years that followed.

April Revolution

After Trujillo's death the country predictably fell into political chaos, governed provisionally and briefly by a Council of State whose makeup and status was largely determined by military pressure. Years of pent-up frustration cleared the way for the popular victory of Juan Bosch as president of the republic when elections were finally held in 1962. The leader of the social-democratic Dominican Revolutionary Party (PRD), Bosch had spent many years in exile and promised a government based on justice and reform.

Bosch achieved little, however, and lasted only seven months in office, as military officers loyal to *trujillismo* overthrew his democratically elected government and annulled the constitution. Troops surrounded the National Palace on September 25, 1963 and arrested the cabinet. Three days later Juan Bosch, the deposed president, was exiled to Puerto Rico.

The Triumvirate, a hastily arranged civilian government, was immediately sworn in, although real power remained with the military coup leaders. Two years of ensuing political and economic turmoil led to mounting unrest, the subsequent downfall of the government in April 1965 and the eventual outbreak of civil war. Two factions, temporarily united in their aim of removing the government, were soon at each other's throats. The Constitutionalists, whose popular support came from the PRD opposition and a group of young army officers, sought to re-establish the constitution of 1963 and return Bosch to power. The remainder of the armed forces, joined by those civilians who feared a communist uprising, were alarmed by the Constitutionalists' populist rhetoric. This latter group, the so-called Loyalists, spread rumors of an imminent socialist revolution, while mobilizing a squadron of tanks and bombing the National Palace by air and sea. With memories of Fidel Castro's revolution in Cuba still fresh and reports of a rising tide of socialism about to engulf a second Caribbean state, it did not take long before the U.S. was persuaded to enter the fray.

Fearing that a Constitutionalist victory would lead to "a second Cuba," Washington sought to pursue anti-communism via liberal democratic reform, but only after sending in 42,000 marines, under the guise of defending U.S. citizens in Santo Domingo. To provide a cover of multilateral legitimacy, the OAS agreed to establish an Inter-American

U.S. soldiers search civilians at a checkpoint in Santo Domingo, 1965   *AP*

Peace Force to monitor relations between the Constitutionalist and Loyalist factions and to ease the introduction of a provisional government.

Democracy Within Limits

Dr Joaquín Balaguer won the ensuing elections in June 1966, following a violent electoral campaign during which 350 supporters of Bosch's PRD were killed. Balaguer leaned toward the right wing Loyalist faction, the more acceptable option in U.S. opinion. He had been a close advisor to Trujillo and was titular president at the time of his assassination. Balaguer's style of leadership was authoritarian and paternalistic, taking an exacting interest in all aspects of civilian government. Critics of his first term of office claimed that Balaguer was too much of a *trujillista* who sought to imitate his predecessor by dominating the political process and to manipulate a pliable power base. The main opposition, the PRD, boycotted the 1970 and 1974 elections, amid growing fears of political repression and state-led urban violence conducted by paramilitary death squads. Balaguer nevertheless retained a vested core of support, most notably amongst the traditional elite whose economic interests remained protected and the rural population who had benefited from limited land reforms.

Wary of growing U.S. condemnation of the flawed Dominican political system, Balaguer promised free and fair elections in 1978 and the PRD presidential candidate, Antonio Guzmán, was duly elected to office. The opposition only won, however, despite last-minute military intervention in the vote-counting process when it appeared that Balaguer was likely to lose. International pressure, led by U.S. President Jimmy Carter, forced Balaguer's party to accept defeat, but only after arduous recounts and political maneuvering which allowed Balaguer's supporters to maintain a majority in the Senate. The PRD remained in power for two terms, but the presidencies were troubled by financial turmoil, popular dissatisfaction and personal tragedy. When Guzmán came to the presidency his stated aims were to reduce the power of the military and to eliminate corruption. A month before the presidential elections in 1982, he shot himself after discovering that members of his family, who had positions within the government, had been heavily involved in fraudulent practices. The PRD managed to retain the presidential office at the elections, but the incoming president, Salvador Jorge Blanco, faced a severe economic crisis which led to widespread rioting in 1984.

Back To Balaguer

Prevailing political and economic disillusion paved the way for Balaguer's return to the presidential palace, where he installed himself for the next decade. In 1984 the veteran politician had created a renamed political vehicle, the Social Christian Reformist Party (PRSC) and was ready to stage a comeback. The PRD split over the handling of the economy, leaving Balaguer to win a narrow majority in the 1986 presidential elections, winning his fifth presidential term. He then defeated his principal opponent, Juan Bosch, at the next elections in 1990 amid allegations of widespread fraud. The 1994 elections followed a similar course after Balaguer had decided late in the campaign to stand again. In 1994, the main contenders for the presidency were Balaguer and the late José Francisco Peña Gómez, the presidential candidate for the PRD. Balaguer was adjudged to have won, but further accusations of fraud threatened to paralyze the country with growing popular discontent. An agreement was signed between the political parties which limited Balaguer's term of office to eighteen months, later extended to two years after a political sleight of hand by the PRSC, but with the proviso that Balaguer could not stand for re-election.

Political campaigning in 1994 developed tones of virulent anti-Haitianism. The attack against the darker-skinned Peña Gómez suggested that his alleged Haitian ancestry made him an unsuitable, and potentially disloyal, aspirant for the Dominican presidency. The main complaint suggested that he would support a fusion of Haiti and the Dominican Republic to create a single state, resurrecting fears of nineteenth-century Haitian

Peña Gómez supporter displaying
a campaign poster

David Howard

plans to unite the island. Peña Gómez had suffered racist slurs during the elections in 1982 as candidate for mayor of Santo Domingo, but not to the same extent as he did in the 1994 presidential campaign. An election poll stated that 25 percent of those interviewed would not vote for Peña Gómez because he was "violent and uncontrollable," his allegedly aggressive nature usually being linked to his assumed Haitian heritage. A third of respondents from another poll believed that national sovereignty would be at risk if Peña Gómez became president.

The decisive issue of the 1994 elections, however, was that of electoral fraud. Although the length of presidential mandate was reduced, the results of the elections stood as calculated by the Central Electoral Board (JCE) despite serious reservations among foreign observers and active opposition by non-governmental political groups. The scale of the fraud received international media coverage. The PRD claimed that 150,000 opposition supporters were unable to vote, thanks to irregularities committed by the JCE in favor of the PRSC. The JCE, three-fifths of whom were appointed by Balaguer, gave victory to the PRSC, several weeks after the day of the election, by 22,000 votes. International observers agreed that opposition parties were disenfranchised, supporting the credibility of the claims that fraud had taken place. Less than two weeks before the elections, observers were excluded from the offices of the electoral register for three days; one observer was summarily expelled from the country without explanation. During these days the electronic archives of the voting lists were allegedly altered to the government's advantage. Government supporters were given multiple *cédulas* or voting cards, and opponents were excluded from the electoral lists or intimidated. In several areas, dark-skinned Dominicans or Haitian-Dominicans with legitimate voting rights were prevented from entering ballot stations by the police or military, on the supposition that they would vote against the government.

The apparent level of fraudulent practice was staggering. Due to the exclusion of thousands of voters, the JCE agreed to extend voting hours from six p.m. until nine p.m. on the night of the election, but delayed issuing news of the extension until ten minutes after the polls had concluded. Many stations were kept closed by armed government supporters or by the police. The issue of 225,000 surplus voting cards remained unaccounted for at the time of the elections. Abstention from presidential elections in the Dominican Republic is usually between 27 and 30 percent; in 1994, the JCE reported an abstention rate of 6.3 percent for the whole country. Finally, in eight of the twenty-nine provinces, more votes were cast than were registered on the electoral lists. Excess votes amounted to 36,553, over 14,000 votes more than the stated margin of victory. Despite these contradictions in the JCE's own calculations, the election results were confirmed.

Fraudulent mandates and the exclusion of the majority of the population from state politics has meant that the Dominican political system has consistently lacked credibility and legitimacy. Every presidential election, except the most recent in 1996, has been accompanied by complaints of fraudulent practice. Following international condemnation and the political fiasco of the 1994 elections, the pattern of fraudulent elections had to be broken.

Presidential elections were next held in May 1996, involving a three-way battle between Jacinto Peynado of the PRSC, Peña Gómez of the PRD, and Leonel Fernández of the Dominican Liberation Party (PLD). International observers declared that the elections were free and fair. Balaguer, barred from re-election, refused to support his party's candidate or to vote in the elections. Peña Gómez, despite gaining the greatest number of votes, failed to obtain a sufficient majority for outright victory under the revised constitution, and so entered a second round of elections with the runner-up, Leonel Fernández.

A pact between the PLD and the PRSC was sealed by a remarkable political reconciliation between Bosch and Balaguer. The former had to overcome considerable personal grievances against Balaguer to accept any form of political contract. Fierce antagonists for over fifty years, Bosch had been exiled while Balaguer governed through the years of the *trujillato,* and was then denied power by Balaguer as well as being a victim of electoral fraud for the greater part of three decades. In 1990, Bosch failed to gain the presidency by a margin of 24,000 votes, a result again largely attributed to corrupt electoral practice. Peña Gómez and Bosch, the latter by now 88 years old and suffering from Parkinson's disease, were once close allies within the PRD until Bosch left and formed the PLD in 1973.

Juan Bosch Gaviño

Juan Bosch, perhaps more than any Dominican during the twentieth century, has achieved international recognition in both political and literary circles. He, along with Joaquín Balaguer, stand out as the quintessential *caudillos* of contemporary Dominican politics. Bosch, unlike his erstwhile combatant, has achieved widespread respect and recognition for his literary accomplishments and political skills, while never gaining a full term as president. Even as President of the Republic in 1963, during the aftermath of the death of Trujillo, he was ousted after barely seven months in power by a military coup. Although a distinguished academic and writer, he has consistently failed to exhibit the Machiavellian prowess of his long-term opponent, Balaguer.

Born in 1909 in the town of La Vega, Bosch came from a comfortable middle-class background. From the early years of his education, his showed a great talent for writing. At the age of twenty-four, he edited his first book, *Camino Real*, an anthology of famous Latin American writers. Within three decades, not only would his name be included on an equal footing with these authors, but he would be at the center of his country's turbulent political fortunes. After helping to form the PRD in 1939, Bosch faced exile from the Dominican Republic as an active opponent of Trujillo. His return in 1961, following the assassination of the dictator in 1961, led to his ephemeral presidency.

Bosch spent much of his time outside the country, a recurring theme for his critics, but remained active in national politics until he retired as leader of the PLD (the party that he founded in 1973 following a dispute with his one-time political protégé, José Francisco Peña Gómez) before the 1996 elections. Bosch always retained a strong political following, although perhaps his greatest legacy will be that of his novels, essays and political histories. His *Cuentos*, three collections of short stories written before, during and after exile, have been praised as landmarks of consummate story-telling. His evocative, at times blunt, language grasps the heart and emotions of his protagonist, invariably empathizing with the exploited or weak. The source, many would argue, of his life-long involvement in the popular political struggle.

The motives for the political alliance between Balaguer and Bosch may be questioned, but the outcome was clear. The combined political chicanery of the aging Balaguer and Bosch was more than sufficient to keep Peña Gómez from office. The respective party patriarchs and long-term opponents gave victory to Leonel Fernández and the PLD.

The End of the Caudillos?

Leonel Fernández assumed the presidency in August 1996, replacing Balaguer, who had served as president for 22 out of the past 30 years. The change in the political climate was palpable. The outgoing president, 89 years old, blind and barely able to walk, painted a contrasting picture to the sprightly newcomer. Fernández, 43 years old and educated in New York during his formative years, pledged to open up new ways of government. His party slogan at election time claimed to pave a "new road" forward, away from the vested political and economic interests of the traditional elite. It was this establishment, however, which helped to finance and support Fernández's election pact with the PRSC and his party's subsequent victory over the populist appeal of the PRD. Months before the election campaign began, it was claimed that Balaguer himself had authorized the donation of PRSC finances to fund a highly visible publicity campaign for Fernández. The master *caudillo*, unable to stand in his own right, chose tacitly to support the younger, pliant politician from a rival party, rather than lose control of his party to the political opportunists who lurked in the wings of his party headquarters, waiting to lay claim to his legacy.

Balaguer exhibited all the qualities, not least the vices, of the political *caudillo*. He was the archetypal "strongman," illustrated not only by his orders for the often violent suppression of dissent, but also by his supremely skillful manipulation of the body politic and its various actors. He maintained a regal aloofness, despite intervening with even the minutiae of political dealings, yet continued to be able to rely to some extent on a varied following of poor rural peasants and wealthy urban business interests.

Fernández at first allowed a relaxation of Dominican politics, and a democratic space opened into which popular movements and groups flowed. Seemingly gone were the days of the patriarch, and the shuttered and exclusionary nature of *caudillismo* which the majority had been forced to endure. The initial waves of hope, however, were soon to ebb. Euphoria quickly gave way to disenchantment within the first year of Fernández's presidency, as Dominicans flooded the streets in a series of protests against the cost of living and public services.

The political climate of Dominican society has now opened up and the neo-liberal economic policies of the government are aimed at bringing the country more in line with prevailing trade agreements and regional cooperation. Unlike Balaguer, the new president is keen to be seen as a regional figure, traveling throughout the Americas in a flurry of conference visits. Yet Fernández cannot escape the tradition of political patronage. Within days of his inauguration, the national palace was besieged with irate party supporters, demanding the state jobs that they perceived to be their due for voting for the PLD. Political traditions in the Dominican Republic die hard, to which Balaguer himself is living testament.

3   THE ECONOMY: BITTER-SWEET FORTUNES

The hustle and bustle on the streets of Santo Domingo masks the frailties of a national economy that continues to depend on external interests and foreign capital. Over a third of the population lacks secure employment; the affluent gloss of the shopping-mall windows hides the day-to-day desperation which confronts the majority. Dominicans have become used to surviving on the insecurities of the informal economy. Side-street entrepreneurs, the *chiriperos*, hunt for bottles to recycle or peddle an eclectic mix of foods, shabby jewelry or electrical goods. Women domestic servants work a double day's duties as employees and as managers of their own households.

The World Bank estimated in 1992 that 60 percent of Dominicans were living in poverty, a substantial increase from the impoverished 25 percent of the mid-1970s. Successive Dominican governments have been unable to reduce unemployment and unable to meet the demands of a steadily growing population, 60 percent of which now live in urban areas. Inequalities within society continue to worsen. Today, the poorest 20 percent of the population still receive under five percent of the national income. The long-standing gap between rich and poor is nowhere more obvious than in the ongoing dominance of the traditional oligarchy, which has managed the economy according to its needs since colonial times. A handful of family names consistently do the rounds in business, political and cultural circles. The old oligarchy, traditionally concentrated in Santiago, has expanded its interests from the canefields and coffee holdings into export manufacturing and tourist capital. The Barceló, Bermúdez and Jiménez clans wield formidable financial muscle and political clout in a range of public and private arenas.

The Dominican economy has struggled through periods of colonial neglect, the vested interests and internecine conflicts of the landed elite and the zealous personal aggrandizement of a 32-year dictatorship. Much of the Dominican economy was nationalized by Trujillo, to the benefit of his personal coffers. Trujillo's time aside, the dominant influences on the Dominican economy have been those of foreign intervention and growing national debt.

Under Spanish rule, the colony declined from being the "capital of the Indies" to become a forgotten cattle-ranching backwater. The independent nation's fortunes rose through a late nineteenth-century sugar boom, then slumped as the twentieth century progressed. The late 1960s and early 1970s witnessed a phase of economic growth following the stagnation of

Trujillo's regime and the unrest that came in the wake of his assassination. The 1970s in the Dominican Republic were known as the "miracle years," a period in which the abundance of international loans and high sugar prices were matched only by the extravagance of Balaguer's public spending policy. Dams, bridges, new buildings and monuments were planned and lavishly funded. Rising oil prices, however, stifled the spending spree. The foreign capital flow began to dry up, while the country itself was physically battered by Hurricane David in 1979. Over a thousand people were killed amid widespread damage and disruption.

The large trade and budgetary deficits and heavy debt burden of the 1980s have continued through to the present. The economy today exhibits a three-pronged reliance on tourism, the low-wage electronics and garment manufacturing of the industrial free-trade zones, and the international flow of dollar remittances from Dominican emigrants. The country's four traditional export products (sugar, coffee, cocoa and tobacco) accounted for less than 40 percent of all exports in 1996.

Debt and Adjustment

In the first half of the 1980s, the economy labored under a combination of fiscal and external account problems. Rising poverty, unassailable unemployment and inflation running at over 50 percent became the norm. The external debt more than doubled during the 1980s. Export revenues declined, world prices for export commodities see-sawed and the economy was left open to the vagaries of corporate investment. The government turned towards the International Monetary Fund (IMF) for a cure. The medicine, however, left a bitter aftertaste among most Dominicans.

On the morning of April 23, 1984, Dominicans were reeling, shell-shocked at the overnight sky-rocketing of prices for basic medicines and foods. The government had chosen the Easter weekend to impose price hikes under the IMF-induced austerity measures. Shock turned to anger as incredulous residents grouped at local stores throughout the low-income barrios of Santo Domingo. The wrath quickly spread out from the capital, leaving the nation rocked from three days of civil protest and violence. The final tally of state brutality and public grievance left as many as 112 civilians dead, hundreds more wounded in the streets, and over 4,000 demonstrators imprisoned. The riots sent a clear message to subsequent Dominican governments: ongoing debt was both an economic and social problem, capable of stirring up a volatile cocktail of international pressure and domestic strife.

Failure to meet the IMF targets meant that the austerity program was soon suspended in 1984. A one-year standby loan facility of $78.5 million

Tobacco - one of the traditional exports   *Jean-Léo Dugast/PANOS Pictures*

was negotiated by the Dominican government in April 1985, but the conditions provoked such strong political opposition that relations with the IMF were not renewed for seven years.

An important outcome of dealings with the IMF during the 1980s was the devaluation of the Dominican peso, historically at par with the U.S. dollar. In 1991 a dual exchange rate was established, and the official and commercial exchange rates were unified soon after. This devaluation was critical for the attraction of foreign capital to boost an ailing economy. Foreign-owned industries were drawn to Dominican shores by the reduced costs, as were the growing waves of tourists seeking modestly-priced holidays in the sun. International tourism and export manufacturing were to become the mainstay of the economy, replacing sugar and mining operations.

The debt continued to worsen until international assistance became a necessity. Balaguer negotiated a new agreement with the IMF in August 1991, rescheduling $905 million of debt with the Paris Club in November 1991. The terms included an end to price controls, the balancing of state corporation budgets and an expressed commitment to pay outstanding foreign debt arrears. These stringent conditions led to further civil unrest and strikes in 1991, although not on the same scale as in the previous decade.

High rates of inflation, estimated at over 100 percent in 1990, for instance, were crippling the majority of Dominican households at the start of the 1990s. Inflation had worsened in the 1980s due to extravagant government spending on building projects, but lessened by the mid-1990s with the curtailment of public construction and the limited increase of public sector wages. The Central Bank sought to reduce the government deficit and aimed to stabilize the peso against the dollar. At the start of the decade, Balaguer was finally persuaded by international lending agencies and by the Central Bank to reduce spending. Public expenditure was duly cut by a third in two years, leading to further public protest, while government subsidies and social welfare benefits, such as they were, were drastically reduced. Balaguer had previously viewed public expenditure as a key stimulus to economic growth. This had given rise to an overloaded state bureaucracy and a spate of construction proposals, including his *pièce de résistance*, *El Faro a Colón*, a $250 million lighthouse folly in Santo Domingo as a landmark celebration of the five-hundredth anniversary of the arrival of Columbus. External debts with the commercial bank creditors were rescheduled in the mid-1990s and a new standby agreement with the IMF was signed in 1996.

Trade and Aid

Accession to the Lomé Convention with the European Union in 1989 made the Dominican Republic eligible for aid from European funds and allowed duty-free access to the European markets for certain products. Grants worth $115 million were allocated by the EU under the terms of a second protocol to run between 1995 and 2000. The Inter-American Development Bank has also been a major source of development finance. The Dominican government is well aware of the need to retain the confidence of commercial sources and not to jeopardize foreign financial assistance.

President Leonel Fernández has recently expressed the importance of collaboration with regional associations such as the Caribbean Community (Caricom), the Central American Common market and the Rio group. The Dominican Republic has had observer status within Caricom since 1984, and significant commercial relations have developed in recent years. The Dominican Republic annually exports $10 million of goods to Caricom, while buying imports worth $18 million.

Yet despite growing ties within the Caribbean, Dominicans have long considered themselves as Hispanic, expressing a closer cultural affinity to Spanish-speaking Latin America, Cuba and Puerto Rico, rather than the anglophone-dominated Caribbean associations. In 1997, Fernández caused comment among Caricom members by attending Bill Clinton's Central

Aerial view of *El Faro a Colón*, Santo Domingo   *Jeremy Horner/Panos Pictures*

American summit in Costa Rica, rather than aligning himself with the Caribbean leaders at the U.S. president's Barbados summit.

Multilateral donors such as the World Bank, the United Nations and the European Union hold major stakes in the Dominican economy. Similarly, bilateral donors such as Italy, Japan, Germany, France and Korea are important allies. The U.S., however, remains the major player on the Dominican scene. Nearly 50 percent of Dominican exports find their way to the U.S.; less than 20 percent enter the European market. In terms of imports, 44 percent come from the U.S., 15 percent from the EU, 11 percent from Venezuela, and 4 percent from Japan.

The Caribbean Basin Initiative (CBI), established by the Reagan administration in 1983, singled out the region as an important target for U.S. political and economic interests. Under the terms of the agreement, Caribbean countries were given preferential access to the U.S. market for certain goods. This heightened the attractiveness of the Dominican Republic as a branch-plant economy, a low-cost base from which U.S. firms could manufacture and export their products back to the home market.

The 1994 North American Free Trade Agreement (NAFTA) between the U.S., Mexico and Canada threatened to ostracize Caribbean economies by offering North American corporations preferable investment opportunities across the Mexican border. The Dominican Republic, in particular, was faced with the overnight collapse of its export economy, potentially being left in the cold while U.S. manufacturers migrated to the warmth of a welcoming and cheap-labor Mexico. Tough negotiations eventually led to a series of concessions for Caribbean producers, including preferential market access for certain manufactured goods such as garments — a saving grace for the Dominican economy.

The Dominican economy has by necessity become more outward-looking in the last decade, but remains highly dependent on capital coming from abroad. The government courts the favor of overseas export manufacturers, lures tourists to its foreign-owned resorts and awaits the return of remittance money from its itinerant workforce. Reliance on overseas and bilateral aid has decreased, but the servicing of the external debt, which still nears $4 billion, continues to represent five percent of Gross Domestic Product and 17 percent of income from exports. Debt repayments and falling commodity prices, for ferro-nickel and sugar in particular, have exhausted foreign exchange reserves. A vicious circle of debt ensnares Dominican economic policy. To raise sufficient foreign exchange reserves to pay off tightening debt schedules, the export economy is stimulated by devaluing currency to make Dominican goods and labor more competitive. This serves to increase the cost of imported goods and lower the relative value of workers' wages even further. Popular protests and an unsettling environment for investment are the frequent outcome.

Sugar: Going, Going...

The fluctuations of the sugar market have underpinned the booms and slumps of the Dominican economy since Columbus arrived on his second journey with two bundles of cane. Now, the final curtain could be set to fall on the sugar industry as a major economic performer.

Sugar was first cultivated on Hispaniola at the start of the sixteenth century. By the 1530s there were already six sugar mills and nineteen refineries in the Spanish colony. The initial impetus for production, however, soon became stifled by colonial trade restrictions, which demanded that all commerce be channeled through a single counting house in Seville. Direct trading with any other country was prohibited. Given the limited incentives to expand, sugar output ground to a standstill by the end of the century.

It was not until the end of nineteenth century that Dominican sugar was revived as the country's main export commodity. Cuban immigrants, and later Puerto Rican, U.S., and Italian entrepreneurs, developed a series of modern plantations along the southern coast. Failing sugar prices forced several concerns out of business during the 1920s, and the majority continued to be run by foreign, mainly U.S., interests. The largest sugar

Sugar cane on the road to processing   *Philip Wolmuth/PANOS Pictures*

complex was at La Romana, and was owned by the South Puerto Rico Sugar company until it was bought by the U.S.-based Gulf and Western company in the 1960s.

The Trujillo dictatorship wrought major changes in the ownership of sugar production. A fivefold rise in world sugar prices towards the end of the 1940s caught the Benefactor's attention, prompting him to cash in on an expected cane bounty. By the mid-1950s, Trujillo controlled two-thirds of Dominican sugar production. Following his assassination, these assets were managed by the government-owned State Sugar Council (CEA), which was for thirty years the country's largest sugar producer. In 1993, however, state production of sugar was overtaken for the first time by a private enterprise, the Central Romana Corporation, formerly Gulf and Western, which produced 370,000 tons of sugar compared with 311,000 tons in the state sector. This trend has continued, with Central Romana producing 345,000 tons compared to the CEA's 207,000 tons in 1996. The CEA has received much criticism for poor management and consistently decreasing sugar yields, although the fate of the industry has fallen largely into the hands of external agents and the international market.

Until the mid-1980s, the Dominican Republic was the largest beneficiary of the United States' import quota system which provided a preferential market for over half the country's sugar exports. Major adjustments in U.S. consumption patterns, especially the switch by Coca-Cola and Pepsi to high fructose corn syrup and artificial sweeteners, meant that sugar-cane quotas were slashed. By 1997-8, the Dominican Republic's quota had been reduced to less than 200,000 tons, compared to 535,000 tons in 1983-4.

In 1983, the international price of sugar fell to half the cost of production at a time when sugar accounted for nearly 50 percent of Dominican exports. Price cuts, combined with the reduced U.S. sugar quota, severely diminished export revenue. The sugar industry, and thus the country, were in crisis. Since the end of the 1980s government policy has been to diversify the economy and to lessen the potentially crippling dependence on sugar. Annual decreases in the volume and value of sugar exports and production since 1990 nevertheless continue to cause concern. Such concern reached the level of national outcry in 1992 when it was announced that the country would actually need to import refined sugar for local consumption. Sugar remains the principal crop, contributing $170 million to exports in 1996, but overall production continues to decline. The ailing CEA has been earmarked for privatization, but experts agree that its old-fashioned infrastructure is unlikely to attract investors.

Traditional and Non-Traditional Exports

Other traditional export crops have taken less of a battering. Coffee and cocoa each accounted for $65 million of export earnings in 1996. The Arabica bean was introduced to Hispaniola during the mid-eighteenth century, and although coffee is traditionally cultivated on family-based smallholdings, its exportation continues to be dominated by eight family firms. The collapse of the International Coffee Agreement (a system of quotas to ensure stable world prices) in 1989 led to a marked reduction in profits, although output has begun to rise in recent years.

Cocoa was first planted by Spanish colonists in the sixteenth century. Similar to coffee production, plots tend to be small and producers dependent on merchant middlemen. Three large exporting houses account for four-fifths of overseas trade. The importance of the coffee and cocoa production during the last century created an influential merchant class in the Cibao, and laid the basis for the region's early dominance in national affairs.

Tobacco, which has the longest history of all Dominican export crops, remains one of the few traditional products which has encountered a surprising expansion in recent years. An early Spanish colonist singled out the use of the particular weed when describing the imperfections of the indigenous Tainos, which included, "among other vices, one very bad one, which is to inhale smoke, which they call tobacco, in order to make themselves senseless." Despite the existence of a vigorous anti-smoking lobby, the international cigar market is nevertheless expanding. In 1995, 95 million cigars were exported from the Dominican Republic, making it the largest cigar exporter in the world. Dominican cigar producers have benefited from the U.S. embargo against Cuba and the growing popularity of cigar-smoking during the 1990s in the U.S. and Europe. The revenue raised from cigars is now roughly $100 million annually.

Non-traditional crops have grown considerably in importance since the late 1980s. Expanding production of pineapples, bananas, melons, citrus and other fruit, cut flowers and ornamental plants enabled this sector to contribute $186 million to exports in 1995. Nevertheless, total agricultural exports have been outstripped by mining sector exports in recent years.

Buried Treasures

The lure of gold enticed the first Spanish colonists to Hispaniola. Indigenous Tainos were enslaved to work the gold reserves which, despite initial predictions of abundance, appeared to have been exhausted by the 1520s. The Spanish prospectors moved west to the greater riches of mainland America. Mineral extraction then played little part in the Dominican economy until the middle of the twentieth century, but by 1996 accounted for $271 million of all exports. Trujillo, never slow to add to his personal wealth, granted concessions in the 1940s for the Alcoa Company to exploit bauxite reserves in the southwest of the country. The most profitable mining operations, however, have focused on nickel deposits and, since the mid-1970s, on the renewed search for gold.

Falconbridge Dominicana, registered as Dominican but with a Canadian parent company, led the extraction and refinement of the substantial nickel deposits located near Bonao in the center of the country. Reserves in the Dominican Republic have been estimated at ten percent of the global total. Production took off during the 1970s, but under extraction concessions which allowed 80 percent of gross profits to go to the overseas investors. During the late 1980s, the contribution of ferro-nickel production enabled the mining sector to surpass agriculture as the highest export earner. Fluctuating international prices, however, led to a suspension of mining activity in 1993. Despite a renewal of operations in 1994, the vagaries of the international market have continued to undermine the stability of ferro-nickel production in the Dominican Republic.

In their haste to track down the promised El Dorado of mainland America, the early Spanish colonists passed over what is now one of the largest gold mines in the western hemisphere. The riches of the Pueblo Viejo mine in the vicinity of the ferro-nickel deposits at Bonao were discovered in the early 1970s. Since then, gold and silver mining has made an important contribution to the Dominican economy. The U.S.-owned mining company, Rosario Dominicana, was nationalized in 1979 in an attempt to gain greater control over the profits of gold extraction. Yet high running costs and accumulated debts, the exhaustion of gold and silver deposits at the upper levels, plus claims of mismanagement, forced the state mining company to suspend its operations at Pueblo Viejo in 1993. Since re-opening in 1994, reserves have been estimated at 550 million tons of gold-bearing ore and export profits have risen.

The problems of the mining industry have not been restricted to economic management, productivity and international price fluctuations alone. There is mounting concern over the immediate and long-term effects of the environmental pollution associated with mineral extraction. Heavy metal contamination of outwash from the Rosario Dominicana mine has poisoned the waters of the River Chacuey in the Zambrana. Local residents have been relocated from several areas where the level of air- and water-borne contaminants reached dangerous levels in the 1990s.

The Blue Jean Economy

Since the mid-1980s, the Dominican economy has been radically reshaped by the arrival of two new groups: export manufacturers and tourists. The advent of both sectors is primarily related to the devaluation of the peso. Structural adjustment led to a currency devaluation which reduced the basic cost of labor to around 50 cents per hour at the start of the 1990s. The Dominican Republic became a cheap place in which to produce and play. Both sectors are concentrated in specific locations, manufacturing within the demarcated industrial free zones, and tourism within the fenced-off resort complexes along the coast. The export manufacturing industry was also encouraged by U.S.-led plans for a regional market. The Caribbean Basin Initiative gave U.S. clothing manufacturers tempting tax initiatives to locate their production in the country. As a result, garments are now the main export of the Dominican Republic.

Industrial free zones are the country's third largest employment source, after the public sector and the sugar industry. There were 40 industrial free zones located around the country at the end of 1997, housing 446 companies and employing 182,000 people. Employment in the export manufacturing industry largely explains the fourfold increase in female employment rates from nine percent to 38 percent since 1960. Women account for 60 percent of workers within the trade zones, a result of traditional gender perceptions which see women as being more suited to certain tasks involving manual dexterity and patience. Two-thirds of exports consist of garments and textiles, although footwear, leather goods and electronic components are also important products. Women are employed primarily in unskilled production, whereas managerial positions are predominantly filled by men. Women's wages tend to be lower than their male counterparts and unionization has traditionally been weak due to fragmentation and the importance given to political party affiliation. Workers can expect ten-hour shifts with a short mid-morning and a half-hour lunch break for a monthly wage of $80-$120. Supervisors may earn up to $350 per month.

Just Do It: A Day in the Free Zone

The day begins at 5 a.m. Coffee to brew, the remnants of last night's rice and pastelitos to rejuvenate for the family breakfast. Although you're living through days of tropical heat, there's still a chill in the dawn air and the damp freshness of a new day. The 40-minute trek by screeching *guagua*, one of the capital's rust-ridden fleet of aging minibuses, lands you at the perimeter fence of the industrial free zone, just along from Santo Domingo's international airport. As the early morning charter flight arrivals are rapidly bussed along the adjacent highway to their sunshine resorts, you pour with the hundreds of other women workers through the gates to your white, metal work block. Another eleven-hour day in the factory, behind the same machine, molding the same patches to the same sneakers, waiting for the same 10-minute mid-morning break to grab a few brisk moments of news with the other machinists. When the siren sounds and the foreman yells, sewing machines and presses are once more cranked into life and the deafening noise recommences. During the two-and-a-half-hour slog to lunchtime, the factory warms up with the day's heat and the workshop's activity. Sweat lubricates the ever-present dryness and dust, compounded by the unswept debris of garment cuttings and nonexistent ventilation. The stench of plastic adhesive adds to the dizzy cocktail of hurried production. The end of the half-hour lunch break heralds four more hours of tedium, mental and physical exhaustion, then home. Rice and beans to cook; all for the weekly wage of $20.

The Dominican export-oriented economy requires low labor costs to maintain its place in the regional economy. This has meant that work conditions have deteriorated and are increasingly precarious. Government spending cuts have removed the few programs which focused on education, health and occupational equality. One exception was a new labor code to protect the collective bargaining rights of workers, passed in 1992 but widely ignored by employers. Previously, union membership was discouraged, often via means of dismissal and blacklisting. Companies know that their workers' ranks can easily be filled in an economy where labor supply easily exceeds demand. Many workers accept short-term employment with severance pay, then seek reemployment by the same firm. Companies are thus relieved of long-term welfare commitments.

La Romana electronics assembly plant   *Philip Wolmuth/PANOS Pictures*

Foreign-owned companies dominate the manufacturing sphere. Almost a half of all companies are owned by U.S. or Canadian interests, while a fifth are owned locally. Other countries with investment interests include South Korea and Taiwan. The industrial free zones contributed over $520 million to the national balance of payments in 1996, while enjoying "tax holidays" of up to 20 years, duty-free material imports and a range of financial benefits. Annual exports totaled over $960 million in 1996.

The dangers of an externally-induced export economy appeared ominous even during the early 1990s. Just as quickly as the Caribbean Basin Initiative set up investment opportunities in the Dominican economy, NAFTA looked set to divert them away. Export manufacturers could now locate in Canada or, more importantly, in Mexico and gain preferential access to the U.S. market. The collapse of the Mexican peso in 1995 meant that many companies relocated across the border, with the result that Mexico has now become the leading supplier of garments to the U.S.

The industrial free zones, however, will remain important features on the Dominican economic landscape for the foreseeable future. Not only have they become growth poles of economic policy, but they are also part of the social and even cultural agenda. The government recently announced the creation of three new industrial parks along the Haitian border to develop the local economy and to reduce migration, especially to Santo Domingo. President Fernández has voiced his concern over the depopulation of the frontier and the continued influx of Haitian laborers. Whether these industrial zones serve to strengthen the Dominican economic presence in the region, or merely to attract more Haitian migrants remains to be seen.

"The Best Kept Secret in the Caribbean"

The Dominican Republic arrived relatively late on the tourist scene. Trujillo was never keen to have too many foreigners snooping around his property, and the civil turmoil of the 1960s was clearly not the stuff of Caribbean paradise. Nevertheless, a rapid catch-up act during the 1970s, combined with the currency devaluation of the 1980s, placed the Dominican Republic firmly on the tourist map. The country could now offer prospective visitors the security of a stable democracy, and the standard tropical fare of picture-postcard beaches and year-round sunshine.

Tourism is now the largest source of foreign exchange, with annual receipts exceeding $1,860 million, twice the amount generated by exports. The industry engages about five percent of the labor force in terms of direct employment and associated activities such as service provision and construction. The country now boasts five international airports at Santo Domingo, Puerto Plata, Punta Cana, Barahona, and Samaná. The number of hotel rooms had increased to 35,750 by the end of 1996, with average hotel occupancy rate remaining high at 79 percent. Almost two million visitors arrived in 1996, with charter flights accounting for 680,000.

The tourist industry has focused on the budget end of the market, catering particularly to the all-inclusive package tours from North America and increasingly from Europe. The Dominican Republic is now the most popular Caribbean destination among European tourists, and over half of all British visitors to the region vacation on its shores. Tourism is concentrated in a series of resort complexes, largely owned by foreign companies or Dominican franchise. The nature of the all-inclusive sun, sea and sand package holiday has meant that the tourist seldom ventures beyond the confines of the resort complex perimeter into the interior or cities other than Santo Domingo.

The environmental problems of intensive tourist development have been raised in recent years. The use of pesticides to clear mosquitoes from coastal lagoons, the problem of untreated sewage from resort complexes, and the clearance of forests for golf courses are pressing issues. The Dominican industry is beginning to realize that it can no longer afford to develop in an environmentally unaware void. There is potential for eco-tourism, with fourteen National Parks and seven scientific reserves covering twelve percent of the national territory. Eco-tourist ventures have been proposed for trekking vacations in the interior highlands or around the region of Lago Enriquillo.

Other unwanted aspects of modern tourist development have affected the social environment. There is growing international concern over sex tourism, particularly where it involves the exploitation of minors. The Dominican Republic has become one of the major international destinations for the sex holiday industry. The demand for male and female prostitution in tourist areas has attracted the attention not only of sex workers and clients, but has also provoked attempted government crack-downs and international media coverage. Having worked hard to promote the image of the Dominican Republic as a leading holiday destination, both the government and the main tourist operators are keen to keep it clean. Press reports in early 1998, criticizing Dominican resorts for poor hygiene standards, were another blow to the industry's public relations image.

Remittance Economy

The final piece of the contemporary economic jigsaw arrives by mail. Remittances sent back by Dominican migrants abroad are now crucial to the national economy as a major source of foreign exchange. Estimates placed the value of these remittances at between $230 million and $280 million per year during the 1980s, making them a more valuable source of hard currency than the sugar industry. By 1989, remittances equaled the sum of the three traditional exports from the Dominican Republic: sugar, coffee and tobacco. Today, annual remittances are estimated at $800 million, originating mainly from the U.S. and Puerto Rico. Only the income generated by tourism challenges the importance of migrants' money. The country's second city is not Santiago, but New York. With increasing numbers of Dominicans relying on family and friends working "over there," even Santo Domingo's claim to be the capital seems threatened.

The impact of remittances increased during the 1990s as the Dominican economy deteriorated. Felipe Jiménez, from his patched-up house in one of Santo Domingo's sprawling low-income slum districts, does not consider a job in the Dominican capital sufficient, but aims for New York City: "There you have hope, a chance to get on and get going with your life." He and his family rely on the money sent back by his brother who works ten-hour shifts in a New York bottling factory.

Dependence on migrant remittances is not restricted to the urban majority. Whole villages have become dependent on the labor of their itinerant members. A study in the Cibao region illustrated that one-third of a community's income was generated by remittances sent from the U.S. Most of the money is used for day-to-day expenses; very little is saved.

Remittance checks are often cashed informally, never going via the Central Bank to add to the country's dollar reserve. As a result, the exact influence and size of remittance capital is difficult to ascertain. The

International Labor Organization argues that although remittances selectively help some families, the net positive effects are debatable. Remittances may provide temporary relief for individual families, but, in general, migration has promoted a dependency on these payments which has undermined social and economic structures at home. Inequality among household incomes has increased, and ostentatious displays of wealth among those who have tasted success in the Big Apple are not uncommon. Disparities in wealth have led to a split society, divided between those with access to remittances and those forced to survive without external assistance.

4 SOCIETY AND MIGRATION: BETWEEN TWO WORLDS

"There goes the light!"

"¡Se fue la luz!" has become one of the most common Dominican phrases in recent years, but its popularity is not an expression of happy sentiment. Dominicans live with a perennial power cut. The seemingly endemic failure of the state power company to supply sufficient electricity has become a daily source of debate, complaint and, most recently, popular protest.

Energy-generating operations by the Dominican Electricity Corporation (CDE) have been critically inadequate during the 1990s. Production is often below half of the peak demand. Difficulties are caused by the frequent withdrawal from service of faulty generating units, periods of drought which lower hydroelectric production, and a highly inefficient distribution system through which one-half of electricity produced is lost in transmission or via illegal connections. A tangle of wires criss-crossing overhead to tap the few electricity lines for common use is a frequent sight in the poor neighborhoods of Dominican cities.

During the spring and summer of 1997, Dominican society rumbled under a hovering cloud of discontent, expressed by a series of regional strikes and violent outbursts. Since his election in 1996, President Fernández has faced growing criticism for the failure of his government to provide adequate public services, ranging from power supply and refuse collection to the pricing of fuel and basic foods. The PLD seems to have lost track of the "new path" which was promised in the party manifesto and splashed across billboards throughout the country.

Dominican society has failed to shake off the legacy of discontent dating from the Trujillo years, which found expression briefly during the April revolution in 1965, before being forced underground by the revived repression of the 1970s. Popular demonstrations have continued to echo the tremors of this social and economic unrest. The Dominican Republic is a divided society, continually turning in on itself while reaching for the seemingly golden shores of the U.S. The haves and have-nots may share a culture of *merengue* and MTV, but the wealth gap between the minority of rich and majority of poor has only widened over the last thirty years.

Increased rates of urbanization have fueled the growth of squatter settlements and helped to prepare the way for migration overseas. To have a *dominicanyork* (a Dominican migrant in New York) in the family, has become the most viable means of making ends meet. The Dominican Republic is now a transnational society with over one-tenth of its population living in the United States.

As Dominican society faces the challenges of the coming century, the social problems of a population, about half of whom live in poverty according to national and international studies, seem to worsen. The majority of Dominicans suffer poor housing conditions and lack reliable public services. Over half of the population has no access to the electric grid; those who do have access tend to live in the privileged residential areas of the capital or else endure up to fourteen hours of power cuts a day. The tendency of businesses and wealthy households to make up the electricity shortfall with their own oil-powered generators has visibly increased urban levels of pollution. Poor sanitation and polluted water lead to frequent tuberculosis and typhoid outbreaks, while hospitals face severe shortages of essential drugs and equipment. Less than half of all children are vaccinated against preventable diseases. Endemic corruption, a burgeoning drug trade, widespread prostitution and a high rate of HIV infection add further problems to an already stressful daily reality for the majority of Dominicans.

Popularizing Protest

Social protest has become a recurrent feature of everyday life during the 1980s and 1990s. Whereas political upheaval and liberation were the motives for civil unrest in the 1960s, the extent of the country's economic and social crises more frequently provokes widespread protest today. Two years after the "IMF riots" of 1984, the country was paralyzed as judges, followed by doctors and medical staff, then architects and engineers, went on strike for several months. The anger of popular protest may overflow to the middle classes, although most militant activity is confined to the low-income areas, so-called *barrios calientes* (hot neighborhoods), of Santo Domingo. At the start of the 1990s, labor conflict soared as the economic well-being of the country tumbled. This led to a series of general strikes and subsequent brutal repressions by the Balaguer government.

The popular movement traditionally includes the marginalized sectors of urban and rural society — the young, the elderly, women, and those who gain their livelihood from the unregulated economy, without recourse to formal employment provisions. During tense periods of social unrest, committees for popular struggle evolve in the barrios to coordinate objectives. Collective action focuses on local needs but frequently escalates to national demands. Ongoing popular protest and strikes during the summer of 1997 culminated in the call for a general strike by the Coordinating Committee of Grassroots, Union and Driver Organizations. Wide-ranging demands included a general wage increase, a reduction in fuel prices and in the cost of living, the completion of unfinished public

50

Special forces raid Capotillo district during
the strike in November 1997.

AP Photo/John Riley

works and a solution to the energy crisis. The sheer number of popular
organizations, however, often leads to fragmentation, infighting and limited
long-term planning. In the capital city alone, there are over forty women's
organizations whose purposes are to confront the patriarchal norms of a
machista society. Despite the existence of a central coordinating committee,
much effort is duplicated or dissolved through disputes.

Popular protest movements have formed the basis for the creation of
political parties, usually at the expense of their initially radical nature.
Padre Antonio Reynoso was an outspoken priest, influenced by the ideals
of liberation theology, who approached the 1994 elections as a candidate
with an agenda for radical change. His Independent Movement of Unity
and Change (MIUCA) received much popular support during the election
campaign although few votes. Father "Toño" now holds a position within
the PLD, co-opting MIUCA as a considerably weakened ally of the
government.

Women's Issues

A popular children's song presents an image of women which reproduces
in verse the social structures of patriarchy in the Dominican Republic.
The songwriter sets out his requirements for marriage, the lyrics suggesting

that the ideal wife should be wealthy and skilled at sewing and cooking. She must have all the necessary domestic skills to fulfill the role of a "good housewife." The verses encapsulate the conventional and widespread conception that domestic matters are women's issues. A well-known chain of Dominican supermarkets has recently considered the creation of rest areas, "as an alternative for husbands who become bored in the supermarket, while their wives buy the family shopping." Women, it is argued, take much longer to buy the groceries; men spend more money, and also purchase rum, whisky and snacks to entertain guests at home.

Previous theories of development assumed that urbanization and industrialization would open up social and economic opportunities for women. In objective terms, more women are gaining remunerative employment in the Dominican economy. During the 1970s, women's employment in urban areas increased five-fold compared to male employment rates, while between 1981 and 1990, the female labor force as a whole doubled to over one million workers. In addition, women's employment levels are increasing relative to those of men. The number of women described in the census as economically active over the last decade (which excludes many informal workers, students and women working in their own household) increased from 41 to 55 per hundred male workers.

Whereas more women are actively seeking and gaining employment, many of these jobs are poorly paid or reproduce traditional gender-ascribed tasks such as cleaning, cooking or garment manufacture. An increasing concentration of women, over 50 percent during the 1990s, are employed in the informal sector and domestic service. These sectors have the lowest salaries and minimal legal protection.

It has been argued that the changing focus of social protest movements to issues of infrastructure, water and housing provision places women more squarely at the forefront of popular urban struggle. Women have increasingly taken on the role of community activists and entered the sphere of neighborhood politics, albeit within the existing patriarchal frameworks. *Machismo* remains potent at all levels of social interaction. Domestic violence against women is commonplace and largely ignored by mainstream society. On a national scale, there has been a decline in consensual union and marriage (only 25 percent of partnerships are legally recognized marriages), and this has been accompanied by a rise in the level of divorce or, more commonly, separation. Women have few rights and little chance to exercise them in most cases of relationship breakdown.

Despite persistent differences between rural and urban areas, the birth rate is decreasing steadily. The average number of children born per woman during the early 1960s was 7.3; today the average is 3.3. This reduction has been achieved through extensive family planning programs. The majority of Dominican women now have access to methods of contraception, although male attitudes continue to be a stumbling block. Safe sex practices are frequently treated with scorn by some Dominican men, the use of condoms often being seen as an infringement on male sexual enjoyment. Among sexually active adolescents, a recent survey reported that 87 percent did not take precautions against contracting HIV and other sexually transmitted diseases. Family planning remains very much a "women's matter" (*una cosa de mujer*) throughout Dominican society.

Nevertheless, traditional domestic codes are slowly being challenged by the increasing numbers of women who have undertaken paid employment outside the home. The position of women workers still remains subordinate to that of men overall, but gender relations within the household have been modified. Changing daily routines, varying forms of household structure and new patterns of earning are beginning to alter relationships inside the home.

Human Rights

Given the propensity for popular protest and the legacy of a 32-year dictatorship, it is not surprising that the Dominican police and military forces have developed a reputation for, and undoubtedly an experience of, repressive tactics. In 1996 the National Directorate for Drug Control (DNCD) was held responsible by human rights activists for 35 extra-judicial killings. Human rights activists themselves have been targets of government intimidation and dubious judicial process. Over 90 percent of the inmates at the country's largest and most notorious prison, La Victoria, have never been tried in court.

The Trujillo regime marked the zenith of human rights violations during the modern era. Repression and violence were inherent in the dictatorship. In 1937, the long-standing hatred and fear of Haitian immigration led to the massacre of approximately 15,000 Haitians and Haitian-Dominicans, and the deportation of thousands more. The expulsion of Haitians continues today; during the 1996 election period, 3,000 Haitian workers, many of whom were legal residents, were expelled from Dominican territory. The slave-like living and work conditions of Haitian laborers in the sugar industry have been the subject of human rights concern and international complaint from the 1970s until the present day.

Most of Trujillo's victims were opponents, real or imagined, to his absolute control of the country. His brutality, however, was not restricted by national borders. In 1956, the assassination of Jésus de Galíndez in New York, a Spanish exile who had just completed a thesis which criticized the

Juan Bosch returning from exile, 1965

Trujillo regime, gained international notoriety. Also, Trujillo's attempt to assassinate Rómulo Betancourt, the president of Venezuela, led to worldwide condemnation and CIA involvement in his own downfall.

President Balaguer was not slow to use coercive tactics and force. He curbed opposition through co-option, discrediting his opponents and sending many into exile. His main opponent, Juan Bosch, went into voluntary exile as a result of political repression and threats on his life. During the 1966 presidential elections, he had been unable to conduct a political campaign beyond daily radio broadcasts, while Balaguer had been able to tour the country. The second Balaguer administration gave rise to heightened repression, and the 1970 elections were carried out in an atmosphere of violence. La Banda, a group of government-sponsored thugs, carried out 190 political assassinations between 1970 and 1972. Police harassment of political opponents continued unabated. In February 1973, fears of a Cuban-backed invasion led to the suspension of the constitution and the closure of media outlets. The Autonomous University of Santo Domingo (UASD), the largest public university, was closed down and at one point surrounded by tanks.

The UASD has long been a center of militant political activity. In the early 1960s, *La Fragua*, a revolutionary student group, gained considerable popularity and notoriety. There have been regular confrontations between students and the military and the police up to the present day. During the summer of 1997, the university campus was the location for a series of violent clashes.

A nominal freedom of press and political expression exists today, barring occasional incidents. Narciso Gonzalez ("Narcisazo"), a university lecturer, journalist, and strong critic of then-President Balaguer, disappeared in May 1994. And yet, little has been written by Dominicans about human rights violations and censorship during modern times, largely due to the continuing presence and influence of those who were actively involved in the repression of the 1970s.

The Church

The Church has never been a powerful political factor in Dominican society. Trujillo used religion as an instrument of power by strengthening the influence of Roman Catholicism in an attempt to give his regime moral legitimacy. Despite many years of uncritical endorsement, the eventual opposition by the Church to the growing tally of human rights abuses meant that Trujillo never gained his sought-after title of Benefactor of the Church.

Often-quoted figures estimate that over 90 percent of Dominicans identify themselves as Roman Catholic. In terms of practicing worship, how-

San Francisco Monastery, Santo Domingo   *David Howard*

ever, the figures are less resounding. Dominican faith and the Church are divided. On one hand, there is a gulf between the so-called High and Low Church, representing the schism between a traditional, conservative institution and the radical popular approach of the Christian "base communities" in low-income areas. On the other hand, the Church endures an uneasy relationship with widespread faith in African-Christian beliefs. This is the realm of *brujería*, where African deities and Christian saints are superimposed and worshipped in a medley of formal and informal practices, garnished with diverse offerings. In addition, the rising wave of evangelism that is sweeping through Latin America has made its impact on Dominican society. Baptists, Adventists and Jehovah's Witnesses now compete with Catholic priests for the urban and rural flock.

Shared Spirits

Vodú or voodoo, according to most Dominicans, is strictly a Haitian vice. Vampires, child sacrifice and violent spirits are largely attributed to the western part of Hispaniola. In border regions it is often said that Haitian women have the ability to fly like spirits. *Brujería*, which allegedly encompasses the less malevolent forms of witchcraft, spiritual magic and worship, is more commonly accepted to have Dominican roots. In reality, there is a strong convergence of syncretic beliefs across the island. These forms of worship, however, have gained greater official recognition in Haiti, and subsequently have attracted more international attention. Syncretic religions are an island-wide phenomenon, with certain sites regarded as being of particular religious importance, such as Arcahaie in southern Haiti.

Brujería incorporates notions of knowledge, fear and respect, ranging from advice with lottery numbers or in issues of love, to the more sinister, though no less common, *mal de ojo*, the casting of an "evil eye," often cited as the root cause of a strange or sudden illness. Much unexpected ill health is deemed to be the result of a malicious spell cast upon an opponent via the medium of the *brujo/a*, a male or female priest.

Many Dominicans are often hesitant to admit publicly to a belief in *brujería*. Such faith is often highly personal, open to ridicule by non-believers and discouraged by the Church. Unlike Haitian voodoo, African-Christian syncretic religions in the Dominican Republic are hidden from general view, although the majority of the population share some form of trust in *los santos*. These are saints of the Catholic Church whose religious characteristics and powers have become fused with African deities, a legacy from the period of slavery. Each saint represents certain emotions or is connected to an occasion, with specific prayers and offerings presented to him or her, usually at a small shrine in the home. Flowers, chocolate, soft drinks and cash all serve to court the spirit's attention and favors. Most believers will single out a particular patron saint for personal protection and spiritual guidance.

The popular deities stem from African and European religious traditions, having characteristics both recognizable and suited to their followers' needs. Anaísa, for example, is the popular goddess of love, fond of drinking, dancing and perfumes. Formerly a prostitute, she is a specialist in matters of love. The Barón del Cementerio is the one of the most widely known *luás*, or gods, in the Dominican Republic. He governs cemeteries, protecting bodies and helping the dead purge their sins. Both spirits, Anaísa and the Barón, have their corresponding Catholic saints, Santa Ana and San Elías respectively, a portrait of whom is usually placed in the home of devotees.

Dominicans from all classes consult the *brujos*. A well-known *brujo* in the rural region of Zambrana regularly receives visitors from the provincial capital of Cotuí. These clients come from all social backgrounds, but most conspicuous are the richer clients who arrive at the priest's isolated rural dwelling in expensive four-wheel-drive vehicles. As Dominican society becomes increasingly separated by the wealth gap between rich and poor, the sacred remains a source of common experience.

Recent decades have witnessed a clear, practical split within the Church, stemming from the rise of liberation theology and radical politics during the 1960s. At one end of the scale, the Church maintains a traditional image and conservative stance. At the other end, a growing base of popular support and grassroots activity has spurred the rise of radical and subversive Christian politics. The established Church has readily entered the politics of reconciliation between political parties, taking on the role of arbitrator. During the run-up to the 1994 presidential elections, four out of the five political parties signed an ineffectual "civility pact" in which the Church acted as warrantor. The traditional or High Church, despite claims to the contrary, is essentially seen as *balaguerista*, the religious arm of the former president and the politics of neo-*Trujillismo*.

The weakness of the Church in social and political matters is exemplified by its consistent and ineffectual protests against divorce laws. The Dominican Republic, meanwhile, has acquired more legislation facilitating divorce than any other country in Latin America. Nevertheless, the Church has made an important contribution to public health and education, providing an essential backbone of welfare provision in the face of government shortcomings.

The Armed Forces

The military has traditionally been highly politicized. Its roots lie in the 1916-1924 occupation by U.S. marines who trained a formidable National Guard, later co-opted to powerful effect by Trujillo, a former officer. The armed forces were the key to a dictatorship of violence and coercion. Military officers enriched themselves while the regime enjoyed 30 years of impeccable political stability. At the time of Trujillo's death, defense expenditure accounted for 36 percent of the national budget. Balaguer, like a good apprentice to the master, learnt the art of Trujillo's politics and maintained the armed forces as an over-staffed but loyal adjunct to his subsequent governments.

Such loyalty exhibited itself in the 1978 elections when a group of officers, fearing correctly that Balaguer was about to lose, intervened in the electoral process by closing polling stations and halting the vote counting. The military, however, have their own agenda, of which all Dominican presidents are more than aware. In 1974, when an opposition candidate for the presidency was detained, at a press conference an officer responded bluntly to journalists, curious to establish the legal basis of the detention: "The constitution is one thing; the military another." Nevertheless, the armed forces have generally operated as an instrument of the economic and political elite. With generals highly represented in

Balaguer's administrations, the problem facing Leonel Fernández on becoming president was how to deal with the military top brass and their enhanced pay packets. The military share of government spending during the 1970s had escalated to over 45 percent. This was clearly an unacceptable figure for the cash-starved and IMF-monitored economy of the 1990s. With the process of democratic consolidation underway, the direct impact of the armed forces in political life has been moderated, but military and police uniforms maintain a powerful and visible presence in the corridors of the presidential palace.

Corruption

Corruption is a daily part of Dominican life. While street solicitors busily fleece tourists outside the cathedral in Santo Domingo, the less upstanding members of the public administration are rearranging the treasury's coffers to the benefit of their private accounts. For most Dominicans, corruption is an inevitable aspect of political and social exchange. At one level, it is seen as an entrepreneurial skill; at another, it is the shameless face of government. For all his political vices, few would criticize Balaguer for gross self-enrichment, although financial bribes and pay-offs were undoubtedly a part of his Machiavellian political style. The names of the two previous PRD presidents, however, were synonymous with ill-fated and corrupt governments. In 1982, Antonio Guzmán shot himself in the presidential office after it was revealed that members of his family were deeply involved in fraudulent practices after he had been elected on a firm anti-corruption stance. In July 1988, his successor, Salvador Jorge Blanco was found guilty of illegal arms dealings. In the wake of such events, the Dominican population has lost faith in propriety in public life. Political culture is rife with corruption, none more evident than in the country's long record of fraudulent presidential elections. The 1996 presidential elections were the first to occur in the modern era without claims of widespread fraud — some would argue the first in Dominican history.

The Dominican Republic increasingly acts as a bridge for the shipment of drugs from South to North America. The growing incidence of violent crime on the streets of Santo Domingo is often attributed to the increasing number of Dominicans deported for criminal offenses in the U.S., who then ply their new-found skills and experience at home. The Dominican drugs trade is big business. Given endemic corruption throughout public and private sectors, the ideal location of the country as a staging post, and the ready access to established contacts, it is not surprising that the international narcotics trade feels quite at home. In 1995, the Inspector General of the DNCD was arrested with another military officer for drug trafficking. They were discovered in the quiet rural town of Baní with 250 pounds of pure cocaine.

A Transnational Society

Santo Domingo is a two-hour flight from Miami and three hours from New York. The Dominican population is on the move. Dominican communities have established themselves in countries across the world — in Puerto Rico, Haiti, Venezuela, Spain and the Netherlands, for example — but the U.S. remains the most common destination. The Dominican Republic supplied more new emigrants to New York City than any other country during the 1980s; over half a million Dominicans now live in the U.S.

Migration has dramatically shaped Dominican society over the last three decades. The Dominican Republic has become a transnational society which increasingly relies on migrant remittances and commerce. The growth of Dominican neighborhoods, such as Washington Heights in New York, has made a visible impact on the North American urban and cultural scene. Migrants, who had previously lived by Dominican conceptions of ethnicity and forms of social interaction, faced a whole new set of challenges across the water. For many, the adjustment to a new "Black Hispanic" identity and the upheaval of family networks have been unsettling experiences.

The incorporation of the Dominican Republic into the periphery of the world economy in the late nineteenth century established the basis for the migration of Dominican labor overseas. The U.S. has been the major destination for Dominican migrants during the twentieth century, in particular after the 1960s. During the Trujillo era international migration was limited with fewer than 10,000 Dominicans reaching the U.S. during the 1950s as the regime restricted migration in order to maintain control over the domestic labor force. Following the assassination of Trujillo, restrictions were lifted and the number of Dominicans migrating grew rapidly. Between 1960 and 1963, documented Dominican migration to the U.S. increased from just over 5,000 to 67,000. The Dominican government perceived migration as a necessary and obvious safety valve to relieve social and economic pressures.

The domestic political situation prompted further migration in 1966 and 1978. Both years marked political turning points, when a change of government provoked the emigration of political opponents. The number of legal visas issued in 1966 increased by 74 percent to 16,503, compared with 9,503 during 1965, the year of the April Revolution and subsequent U.S. invasion. Those who feared repression as a result of their opposition to the new Washington-backed government paradoxically found themselves

A *botánica* in New York City

Julio Etchart/Reportage

seeking exile in the Dominican community of New York. The PRD election victory in 1978 was another pretext for politically motivated migration. A deteriorating economy, the prospect of a more radical government, and changing networks of patronage following three terms of PRSC government induced a 60 percent increase in legal residency applications and approvals.

Migration to the U.S. has continued to grow in scale and importance. Dominican nationals are now second only to Mexicans among arriving Latin American nationals; since the 1970s the number of immigrant and non-immigrant Dominicans arriving every year has averaged 150,000. Between 1961 and 1981, 255,578 Dominican immigrants legally entered the U.S., but many more found their way into the country by other means. Legal migration increased by 13.2 percent between 1993 and 1994 to 51,047. The importance of undocumented migration is clear if estimates of up to 1.5 million living in the U.S. today are to be believed, although the figure probably lies at around 800,000. While an exact total remains elusive, Dominican neighborhoods are evidence of the scale of the migratory flow, especially in New York, the destination for approximately 90 percent of Dominicans. Over 50 percent of Dominicans living in the city reside in the north Manhattan area of Washington Heights, a highly visible enclave. There are an estimated 20,000 Dominican-owned businesses in New York, with Dominicans owning approximately 70 percent of the city's small grocery stores or *bodegas.*

Uptown Caribbean: Dominicans in New York

New York City is the largest city in the Caribbean diaspora. Thousands of first-time migrants, regular travelers and U.S. residents pass through the gates of JFK airport every year on the way to or from the island territories. Dominicans, perhaps more than any of the region's traveling populace in recent years, have established their own neighborhoods and set up shop amid New York's varied apartment buildings. Washington Heights, on the Upper West Side above Harlem, has been the site for the growth over the last three decades of a bustling Dominican business and residential enclave.

Emerging from the subway at 181st Street, a North American, metropolitan version of Santo Domingo soon greets the newcomer. Nationwide chain stores display a Dominican flavor on their shelves, catering for national tastes which have been transported from the Caribbean, occasionally reworked, and served up as local. More apparent are the ranks of jewelers selling small mountains of gold bracelets, rings and necklaces — sure investment against the vagaries of bank interest rates and a visible sign of success. *Bachata, merengue* and *salsa* pound out from the plethora of music stores with hot new numbers from Fernandito, Las Chicas, and Raulín, most of which have been recorded in New York studios. *Colmados* or corner stores offer bottles of Brugal, Barceló and Presidente, crusty mounds of *pan de agua* and boast the cheapest direct calls "back home" in town. Finance houses advertise the most efficient routes for the return flow of savings and remittances to family and friends still on the island. Washington Heights and, to some extent, the Dominican community have become tainted by the activities of the drug trade, but more legitimate business activity occurs aboveboard than those who promote the stereotypes would care to admit. A growing number of local entrepreneurs have now successfully devoted their attention to city politics. Dominican voices are beginning to be heard in City Hall, beyond the streets of the so-called Quisqueya Heights.

By the start of the 1990s, the impact of transnational migration was evident throughout Dominican society. International migrants made strong impressions not only as consumers and investors, but also by influencing popular culture, the arts, music and media. The reaction of non-migrants to returnees in rural and urban areas also became more diverse, reflecting their perception, often grossly stereotyped, of North American lifestyles and influences.

During the 1960s and early 1970s, the image of U.S.-based migrants was generally positive in the Dominican Republic, as they were perceived as pioneers, saving diligently for their return to the Dominican Republic and living frugal lives. Migration provided the possibility to increase income earning and social standing, and to improve opportunities for dependents. As the 1970s progressed, however, an increasingly hostile reception was given to returned Dominican migrants. The image of the majority as honest and

61

Queuing for a visa   *Julio Etchart/Reportage*

hardworking became tarnished. The ostentatious display of wealth by some returnees, combined with the growth of the drug trade among some Dominicans in New York, sullied previous perceptions. Dominican migrants are now commonly associated with drug dealing. The head of the North Manhattan drug squad commented, "It is unfair to assume that all Dominicans peddle drugs... although 18 months in the drug trade will earn you enough to go back to the Republic." Social problems in Dominican society were increasingly blamed on influences brought to the island from the U.S.

During the 1990s, the non-migrant Dominican elite, who felt challenged by the younger migrant generation of *nuevos ricos*, promoted images of these migrants as villains, involved in illicit trading, generating inflation, crime, violence and drug problems in the Dominican Republic. Everyday language incorporates disparaging epithets such as *dominicanyork* and *cadenú*, the latter term referring to the extravagant gold jewelry often worn by Dominicans who have lived or still reside in New York. Many lamented the crass materialism that the migrants blatantly displayed, combined with their apparent rejection or loss of *dominicanidad* or Dominicanness; they were, according to critics, neither Dominican nor American.

Visa For a Dream

The illegal or undocumented nature of many migrants' movements between the U.S., Puerto Rico and the Dominican Republic has contributed to their negative image. To enter legally into the U.S., a valid immigrant or temporary visitor's visa is required, making the visa a potent icon and status symbol in Dominican society. There is a general saying: "To have an American visa is to have a profession."

Popular folklore has evolved around methods of visa application. There have often been rumors which circulate in rural and urban areas concerning the latest scam or shortcut in the application process. One story involves the "Day of Grace" in November 1966 when Thanksgiving and the anniversary of President Kennedy's assassination coincided. The size of the queue for visa applications outside the U.S. consulate in Santo Domingo increased fivefold to over a thousand people after a radio announcement reported the unrestricted issuing of visas. The importance of an American "friend" putting in a good word for a visa applicant is also part of the visa folklore, which illustrates the prominence of paternalism in Dominican culture.

Visas have become increasingly difficult to obtain, hence the dramatic rise of illegal migration. The difficulty of obtaining an immigrant visa in Santo Domingo has meant that many Dominicans apply for temporary visas and overstay the legal visiting period. Formal and informal businesses have responded to the demand for visas or illegal entry into the U.S., and agents, brokers and lawyers have all gained financially from the aspirations of potential migrants. In Santo Domingo, a legal consultancy now advises clients specifically on how to obtain residency in the U.S. Brokers, or *buscones*, arrange undocumented entry via Puerto Rico, making use of Puerto Ricans' U.S. citizenship to pass through mainland migration control with the aid of false Puerto Rican identity. The passage to Puerto Rico is usually by boat, or sometimes light aircraft, and Dominican newspapers regularly carry reports of failed attempts, involving the deportation or death by drowning of would-be migrants. Puerto Rico is the second most popular destination for legal and undocumented Dominican migrants, with about 60,000 Dominicans living there. Other undocumented entry routes to the U.S. are via Mexico or the U.S. Virgin Islands.

The importance of migration in Dominican society is illustrated by the relative success of the country's two most recent films to have gained international recognition. *El Pasaje de Ida* (1991) is based on the true story of a dozen Dominican stowaways who hid in the ballast tanks of a Puerto Rican ship, later drowning when the tanks were flooded. *Nueba Yol* (1995), the colloquial Dominican name for New York, recounts the life of Balbueno, a Dominican migrant, who struggles to find work, but eventually makes a successful return to the Dominican homeland. Heavy with stereotypes, the film attempts to portray the contradictions within a migrant's life — the support and demands of kin, the stresses placed upon Dominican family values, the limited opportunities for employment, the insecurity of undocumented status, and the struggle to return home.

5   CULTURE AND IDENTITY: BLACK AND WHITE ISSUES

Popular culture juxtaposes the allegedly white, Hispanic and Catholic culture of the Dominican Republic with the African ancestry, voodoo, and presumed barbarity of its Haitian neighbor. The "Haitian problem" arises from the ongoing antagonism between the two countries, sustained by two centuries of history, and by the increasing numbers of Haitian laborers in the Dominican Republic. Haitian sugar-cane workers, initially contracted by the Dominican government, live in conditions of reputed slavery, arousing intermittent international outrage. Dominican society is an increasingly complex mix of Haitian immigration and Dominican emigration, placed in a culture of fusion: North American fast food, rap and baseball merging with *sancocho, merengue* and *bachata.*

"The Haitian Problem"

The manner in which "Dominicanness" has been portrayed in relation to Haiti has colored, or perhaps more accurately bleached, the image of the Dominican nation. Two processes have operated historically at popular and governmental levels. Firstly, there is one of *blanqueamiento* or whitening, either by encouraging European immigration, for example during the 1930s, or by maintaining a social and cultural white bias. Secondly, the Haitian population is officially and popularly depicted as a threat to the Dominican nation.

In 1983, Joaquín Balaguer, temporarily outside the presidential palace, published a remarkable book, *La isla al revés*, now in its sixth edition and still a best-seller, in which he outlines his hopes and fears for the Dominican nation. The account is a monument to the prejudice and fear that Haiti, as an African-Caribbean nation, instilled in Balaguer and Dominican society at large. The book warns of Haitian imperialist designs which today represent "a plot against the independence of Santo Domingo and against the American population of Spanish origin." Balaguer argues that Haiti is a threat primarily for "biological reasons," voicing opinions which must be considered offensive and disgraceful for a head of state. His polemic is largely constructed of the most banal clichés of racism, such as: "The Black... left to his own instincts and without the restraints which higher living standards impose in all countries on reproduction, multiplies nearly as rapidly as plants."

Leonel Fernández has expressed his intention to improve relations with Haiti, distancing himself from the former policies of Balaguer. However, the deportation of Haitians in the Dominican Republic was re-intensified within months of his inauguration as president. Between November 1996 and January 1997, 15,000 Haitians and Dominicans of Haitian descent were deported during a renewed wave of government activity. Up to 20,000 more were expelled from the Dominican Republic between January and March 1997. The government claimed that it had exposed a Haitian mafia organization devoted to the smuggling of migrants.

Given their shared border, there has been a long history of migration between the two countries. Haitian migration to the Dominican Republic grew in influence during the nineteenth century with the introduction of agro-export capitalism and the development of the modern sugar industry from the 1870s onward. The Haitian presence in the Dominican Republic increased noticeably during the early twentieth century as a result of contract work on the sugar plantations. Following the sharp fall in world sugar prices in the 1920s, Haitian laborers began to replace the existing workforce on the plantations which consisted to a large extent of migrant workers from British territories in the Caribbean. As the Depression hit the entire region's economy, Haitians were prepared to work for much lower wage rates than cane-cutters from islands such as St. Kitts. The number of Haitian workers substantially increased during the U.S. occupation of the Dominican Republic (1916-1924) and Haiti (1915-1934).

Estimates vary widely for the number of Haitians living in the Dominican Republic today. Some suggest up to 1.5 million, but there are probably no more than around 500,000 Haitians and Dominicans of Haitian descent living on Dominican territory. Even so, the size of the population of Haitian origin in Dominican Republic is said to have doubled in the past ten to fifteen years. A quota system in which the Dominican government paid the Haitian authorities for each Haitian worker existed up until 1986. It continues to operate today, albeit informally or via agreement and payment between the countries' military forces. The Haitian sugar workers live mostly in rural communes, called *bateyes*, under conditions so primitive they have been equated with slavery by international human rights organizations.

Living quarters, often grouped as barracks, are usually overcrowded with limited access to adequate sanitary and health services. There are high rates of preventable disease and very poor access to potable water. The rural communities tend to be physically isolated from modern amenities, with limited access to transportation. To attend school, children of Haitian parents must register as Dominican citizens. Lack of

DOMINICAN REPUBLIC
PRODUCING THE GOODS

The local *colmado* (grocery store)
with a wide selection of rums
James Ferguson

Streetside fruit and vegetable
sales in Santo Domingo
Jean-Léo Dugast/PANOS Pictures

Fishing *yolas* rest easy under the
morning sun, Bayahibe
Jean-Léo Dugast/PANOS Pictures

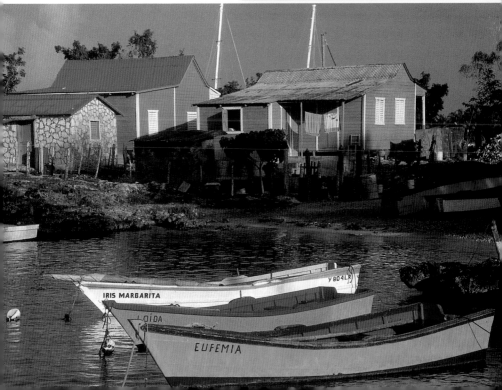

La Ciénaga, low income city living,
Santo Domingo

David Howard

Beachside
restaurant, Las
Terrenas

Jean-Léo Dugast/PANOS Pictures

Rural dwelling, Zombrana

David Howard

Colonial residence, the Alcázar
de Colón, Santo Domingo

James Ferguson

BUILDING STYLES

The presidential palace,
Santo Domingo

James Ferguson

High income homes, Santiago
de las Caballeros

David Howard

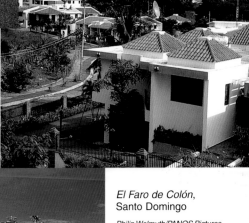

El Faro de Colón,
Santo Domingo

Philip Wolmuth/PANOS Pictures

Coconut harvest
James Ferguson

Flame trees in full bloom
Jean-Léo Dugast/PANOS Pictures

The palm-lined River Chavón flows
below Altos de Chavón
James Ferguson

documentation sometimes hinders the ability of children of Haitian descent to attend school where there is one available. Some parents fail to seek documentation for fear of being deported. Required documentation is often not feasible or impossible to obtain.

It is estimated that 75,000 Haitians work on the sugar plantations, although migrants increasingly find employment outside the industry. A growing proportion of them have been incorporated into coffee production, heightening the dependency of the Dominican economy on Haitian workers. A recent survey of Haitian labor suggested that while under 20 percent of migrants worked in the sugar industry, 8.3 percent were employed in the construction industry, 8.3 percent in commerce and 7.2 percent in domestic service. The remaining Haitians, comprising over half of the migrants, work largely in the informal sector or are otherwise employed in positions which do not highlight their illegal status. The residence of Haitians in the country, the indeterminate nationality of their offspring (without Dominican or Haitian citizenship) and the scale of undocumented immigration are highly emotive issues.

Haitians are perceived by many Dominicans to be totally alien, with Haitian culture representing the very antithesis of Dominican hispanidad and Catholicism. Haitians are commonly linked to voodoo or "black" magic. Few Dominicans have grown up without hearing private or public defamation of the neighboring country. Haitians are popularly scapegoated as the harbingers of moral and physical decay, and their presence is blamed for the existence of malaria in rural settlements and the spread of AIDS.

In July 1997, the UNESCO Committee on Economic, Social and Cultural Rights chastised the Dominican government for "a consistent pattern of disregard for its obligations under the Covenant [on Economic, Social and Cultural Rights] and an unwillingness to co-operate." The Committee was particularly concerned about the exploitation of Haitians, their unacceptable living conditions in the *bateyes*, the arbitrary confiscation of their identity cards and illegal deportations.

Anti-Haitianism was the major stimulus for the deportation, decreed by Balaguer in June 1991, of all undocumented Haitian immigrants aged under 16 or over 60. Within three months, around 50,000 Haitians had been rounded up and deported by the Dominican army, or else had left the country voluntarily to avoid maltreatment. There were alleged abuses of human rights by Dominican forces who used violence and split up families. Second-generation immigrants of Haitian descent, though born in the Dominican Republic, were forcibly deported to a country where they had never lived.

Dominican troops gathering for border patrol, 1994   *AP*

During 1994, the political crisis in Haiti became a major issue in the Dominican elections, as anti-Haitian sentiment was fueled by fears of an "avalanche" across the border. Dominican sovereignty was deemed to be under threat, and Jacinto Peynado, the then vice-president, voiced his concerns over health risks and the spread of AIDS if Haitians were allowed to flee to the Dominican Republic *en masse*. The sovereignty issue was also effectively used by opponents of presidential candidate José Francisco Peña Gómez during the electoral campaign. His alleged sympathies for Haiti and a pact with the exiled Haitian president, Jean-Bertrand Aristide, were questioned, amid claims of an international conspiracy and foreign meddling in Dominican affairs. In 1998, inter-governmental meetings were held, including a summit between Fernandez and Haiti's President Réné Préval, which suggested that long-standing enmities could be resolved, especially with the incentive of European Union cross-border project funding. But among most Dominicans, distrust of Haiti and Haitians is so ingrained that it will take several generations for relations to improve significantly.

Salsa or Burger King?

There is little doubt that the U.S. has been the dominant cultural influence on Dominican society during modern times, increasingly playing the role of *el patrón*, a source of inspiration and consternation reflected by a mixed attitude of affection and antipathy. An ever-present contradiction characterizes Dominican-U.S. relations, expressed in an uneasy balance between an insatiable appetite for North American popular culture and an instinct to blame the White House for much of the country's problems. Dominicans often compare their culture to the national dish *sancocho*: a stew of varied ingredients, mixed and served to taste.

Dominicans share a love-hate relationship with the U.S. in which Dominican culture and sovereignty are waged against the materialism of American life. The latter pays a higher dividend for most aspiring migrants. The wealth of the U.S. compared with the Caribbean region is an overriding factor in people's perception of the country, and the "visa mentality" is a direct response to the perceived gap between North American and Dominican living standards. Many Dominicans seem almost desperate to migrate or travel to the U.S. An often-heard comment laments that Dominican culture is worth little or nothing in comparison with "real" American or European culture. Julia Alvarez, the Dominican novelist, describes the rejection of their homeland by four Dominican women growing up near Boston in the 1960s in *How the Garcia Girls Lost Their Accents* (1991):

> We began to develop a taste for the American teenage good life, and soon, Island was old hat, man. Island was the hair-and-nails crowd, chaperones and icky boys with all their macho strutting and unbuttoned shirts and hairy chests with gold chains and teensy gold crucifixes. By the end of a couple of years away from home, we had *more* than adjusted.

Another of Alvarez's characters is Gladys, a Dominican maid dreaming of migrating to New York. Each icon on her small bedside altar represents a saint. A postcard of the Statue of Liberty has special significance since she is the "powerful American Virgin," the one saint who could send to her to the U.S.

Sovereignty Under Siege

North American influence is pervasive throughout Dominican society. The U.S. embassy in Santo Domingo has been described as the major hub of Dominican politics. A Dominican newspaper suggested sarcastically that President Bill Clinton should have signed the Pact for Democracy between Balaguer and Peña Gómez, the electoral compromise which ended the 1994 crisis. U.S. influence is generally regarded as inevitable, yet fears surrounding the issue of sovereignty have heightened since the U.S. intervention in Haiti. Most governments, however, would be alarmed by the

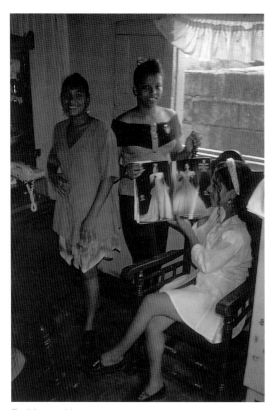

Fashion worlds   *David Howard*

recent comments of a former Assistant Secretary of State for Inter-American Affairs who argued that Caribbean states have little more to offer than sand and "little to export but their populations...While a reversal to full colonial status may be a non-starter...a beneficial erosion of sovereignty should not be." The countries of the Caribbean, he added, "may well be best off accepting and trying to regularize American intervention — as several have now done with regard to the United States Coast Guard and Navy — in exchange for certain trade benefits."

Threats to sovereignty have always been a major issue in the Dominican Republic. The country has been occupied by foreign powers for a total of 35 years since 1822, by Haiti between 1822 and 1844, Spain between 1861 and 1865, and twice by the U.S., from 1916 to 1924 and 1965 to 1966. International agencies and foreign governments have had a significant influence on Dominican affairs for most of the century. As late as 1940, the Dominican customs administrator was an American citizen, nominated by the U.S. president, a hangover from the earlier period of U.S. receivership.

Fears of foreign prying in Dominican affairs are thus long-standing, given the historical precedence of U.S. interest in the region and the recent intervention in Haiti, and the rhetoric of political conspiracy has been rife in the 1990s. In his acceptance speech at the beginning of his eighth term of presidency in 1994, Balaguer warned of dangerous foreign interference in domestic politics. The presidential inauguration was held on August 16, the Day of Restoration, an important public holiday which marks the final withdrawal of Spanish rule in 1865. An outbreak of nationalism, supported by the government, also aimed to deflect attention away from the electoral fraud in 1994. The Nationalist Union, a nucleus of right-wing intellectuals and business people, encouraged a vigorous flag-waving campaign which aimed to promote the fear that the Dominican Republic was about to be overwhelmed by Haitian immigrants and North American politicians.

Although less vitriolic, with no foreign intervention in Haiti or electoral irregularities on which to concentrate, the 1996 elections were again witness to further nationalist rhetoric, again questioning Peña Gómez's suitability to be president. A few days after he had polled the most votes in the first round, opponents called for the creation of a national front to preserve Dominican sovereignty. Leonel Fernández criticized *The New York Times* for suggesting in an editorial that this pact was merely an attempt to defeat a presidential candidate of Haitian origin, while the Secretary General of the PRSC claimed that the editorial itself was part of an international campaign to discredit the Dominican Republic. Dominican newspapers ran a series of articles voicing fears that the nation was in peril.

Concern over growing North American interests in the Dominican Republic has been evident since nineteenth-century critics began to warn of the dangers of economic dependency. After Dominican sovereignty had been lost to the U.S. in 1916, the first military occupation consolidated the process of U.S. capital expansion in the country, and tied the Dominican economy firmly to the North American market. By the 1920s, 95 percent of sugar production was exported to the U.S. and twelve U.S.-owned companies controlled three-quarters of the sugar-producing land. Since the 1920s, over a half of all Dominican imports have come from the U.S.

The effects of U.S. intervention were not only economic. The Dominican language changed during the eight years of occupation as anglicized words entered everyday speech. Baseball replaced cockfighting and soccer as the national sport. Urban elites began to follow North American music styles, but some observers have noted that many Dominicans began to dance *merengue* more energetically as a sign of resistance to the cultural infiltration by American styles. The brief intervention of 1965 reinforced the growing trends of cultural and economic dependency.

Meanwhile, the international migration of labor and capital has placed Dominican society in the growing global economy. The whole range of international relations, through migration, telecommunications, travel, business links, mass media, and the arts, provides an intense and frequent interchange of economic and cultural experiences. Returned migrants share family, friends and business contacts between two or more countries, while still maintaining strong social and cultural links with their country of origin.

Trumpet solo *David Howard*

Merengue *Pop and* Bachata *Blues*

Dominican music, more than any other cultural form, has stood the test of foreign influence. Today, *bachata* and *merengue* retain their dominance, but only just under the challenge of widespread American rock and pop. Open acknowledgment of African influences in Dominican culture is limited, although in most parts the *palo* drums are commonly heard at some stage of a religious ceremony, as are the rowdy processions of the *gaga* celebrations, especially along the western borders.

Two important factors behind the endurance and success of merengue are its Spanish language lyrics and the fact that many *merengueros* have a large Hispanic following in the U.S. and often live there themselves. Transnational commercialization sustains the domestic and overseas strength of the national music, although the emergence of a pop-merengue fusion is evident. North American and European rock and pop have made some inroads into Dominican musical tastes, most notably among the wealthier classes since the 1960s, but the love of Latin-style dancing has maintained *merengue's* popularity. The annual *merengue* festival in the last week of July which sprawls along the seaside Malecón in Santo Domingo is plugged as an event of national significance.

Merengue remains the most distinct type of Dominican music, having developed from European and African origins during the mid-nineteenth century. The traditional merengue band consists of a four-piece group: a *tambora* (small drum), a *güira* (a percussion instrument scraped by a metal rod), a *marimba* (a wooden box with plucked metal keys), and an accordion. In search of unifying and non-Haitian cultural forms, Trujillo aimed to make *merengue* the national music. The country style in particular, *perico ripiao*, from the Cibao region, was upgraded to national status, while the big band sound developed for the dance halls and public functions of Santo Domingo. Horn-based *merengue* soon followed, blaring its way onto the international music scene.

Since the 1970s, *merengue* has moved away from the large band ensembles and speeded up its rhythm, while at the same time reducing the importance of formalized steps. Since the 1980s, Dominican *merengue* has entered a vibrant new era with stars such as Johnny Ventura who led the way with his band and popularized the use of the saxophone. Perhaps the most well-known Dominican musician outside the country is Juan Luis Guerra, who has achieved international success. His music combines *merengue* with a range of other Caribbean and North American influences.

Juan Luis Guerra: Merengue *Maestro,* Bachata *Blender*

Juan Luis Guerra, more than any other Dominican, has grabbed world musical attention. His compositions, especially since the 1980s, have echoed through nightclubs, wafted across the radio waves, accompanied film soundtracks, and, perhaps with less critical distinction but nevertheless a sign of success, molded themselves onto the backdrop of "recognizable tunes" which garnish the foyers and elevators of international hotels. With refined lyrics, synthesized production, an instantly appreciable voice and traditional guitar skills, Juan Luis Guerra has carved his niche with a range of musical styles, most noticeably projecting the sound and image of Dominican *bachata* and *merengue.*

Accompanied by his vocal group 4:40, Guerra has fused sophisticated and inventive *merengue* arrangements with U.S. and Brazilian jazz influences. His album *Bachata Rosa* swept to worldwide success after its release in 1991. Many Dominicans were surprised that a respectable *merenguero* could apparently lower himself to the level of *bachata,* often perceived as bawdy country music. Guerra achieved his success by maintaining the notorious *bachatero's* technique of sexual double entendre, but attuning his lyrical style and composition to a mainstream audience. The range and depth of Guerra's music continues to reach a wide audience. His interests range from sentimental love in songs such as *Burbujas de amor* to the desperate realities of U.S.-bound migration among Dominicans in *Visa para un sueño,* or to *Frío, frío,* inspired by the work of the Spanish poet Federico García Lorca.

Away from the glossy images of fame and fortune, the business interests which direct the music industry have been linked to drug money, while the performances are almost without exception heavily geared towards beer, rum and tobacco promotions. One survey suggests that Dominicans spend on average a third of their income on tobacco and alcohol, which combined with the passion for *merengue* more than accounts for the emphasis given to sponsorship. Dominicans allegedly have the second highest per capita consumption rate of alcohol in the world.

The up-and-coming Dominican challenger to *merengue* is *bachata,* the music of guitar-based ensembles who sing of unrequited love, desire and sorrow, often entwining risqué lyrical twists with the dexterity of their playing. Traditionally, *bachata* was restricted to the tastes of the rural poor, but increasing cityward migration by the peasantry has carried the country rhythms to the urban masses. This music of *amargue,* often expressing the bitterness of life, transcends romantic remorse to recount the frustrations of the urban migrants. Stars such as Luis Segura, Raulín Rodríguez and Tony Santos have taken *bachata* beyond Dominican villages and *barrios* to the international arena. No longer looked down upon as an unfashionable country lament, successful *bachateros* now play to the middle and upper classes of Santo Domingo and New York.

While not originally Dominican, *salsa* has made a great impact on the country's musical tastes and has influenced the style of *merengueros* and *bachateros* alike. The current success of *salsa* dates back to a rise in its international popularity during the 1960s. The source of this promotion arose from the growing number of Puerto Rican musicians in New York who developed the term "salsa" to market a medley of styles and rhythms which displayed a range of emotions from picaresque tales to sentimental romances, and which gave musical expression to the experience of urban latinos.

Dominican Writing

Contemporary literature in the Dominican Republic evolved from a historical background in which European influences were "creolized" in the eighteenth and nineteenth centuries. National versions of contemporary styles, such as neo-classicism and romanticism, formed the basis of literary conventions. As with literary texts and poetry, contemporary Dominican art has largely remained very much aligned to the prevailing European and North American styles.

During the period of Dominican independence in the nineteenth century, the romantic movement had reached its peak in Europe and its influence is evident in the nascent Dominican literature. The early nineteenth century literary scene celebrated the Arcadian forces of nature, which led to *costumbrismo*, the extolling of local culture, customs, flora and fauna. Dominican painting at the time, notably the work of Jaime Colson, Yoryi Morel and Darío Suro, illustrated similar themes.

Local color and the bucolic evocation of a tropicalized Europe were the basis for literary exploration and, in the latter part of the nineteenth century, "indianist" texts developed this rustic style. José Joaquín Pérez glorified the island's indigenous past in *Fantasías indígenas* (1877), while *Enriquillo* (1882), by Manuel de José Galván, responded to the desire to reject an African heritage in favor of a noble indigenous and Hispanic tradition. Galván wrote *Enriquillo* to recount the story of the indigenous leader and archetypal "noble savage" in the former colony of Santo Domingo, who in 1519 led an insurrection against the Spanish colonizers, resulting in peace negotiations with the Spanish authorities. In return for a form of self-government, Enriquillo agreed to pursue and return runaway slaves. Galván describes Enriquillo as a Christian hero, a faithful adherent to Spanish culture and Christianity. *Enriquillo* thus represents the effective syncretism of Spanish civilization and indigenous heritage.

Gastón Fernando Deligne and Fabio Fiallo were the leaders of a Dominican modernist movement at the turn of the nineteenth century, but their work is to some extent overshadowed by the literary historians, Pedro and Max Henríquez Ureña, who were the outstanding writers of their day. In more recent times, Pedro Mir's *Hay un país en el mundo* (1962) and *La isla ofendida* (1965) by Manuel del Cabral addressed Dominican society during the turbulent years of the 1960s.

"Hay un país en el mundo"

Appointed National Poet in 1982, Pedro Mir is widely acclaimed as one of the most influential contributors to Dominican literature. His concern with political and social issues forced him into exile for over a decade during the Trujillo era, and his work has a strong revolutionary content. During the 1940s, Mir's writing was grouped with that of the so-called "Independents," who sought to establish an independent Dominican identity, linking nationalist and continental perspectives. Perhaps his most famous poem, *Hay un país en el mundo* (There is a country in the world), recounts the history of a mythical country, not far removed from the experiences of the Dominican Republic, which has suffered centuries of oppression and exploitation under colonial and autocratic regimes:

There is
a country in the world
                located
on the very route of the sun
Hailing from the night.
                Located
on a dreamlike archipelago
of sugar and of alcohol.
                Simply
weightless,
            like a bat's wing
resting on the breeze.
                Simply
transparent,
            like the trace of a kiss on a spinster
            or the daylight on roof tops
                Simply
fruital. Fluvial. And material. And nevertheless
simply torrid and kicked
in the hips like an adolescent girl.
Simply sad and oppressed.
Sincerely agrarian and unpeopled.

After writing this poem during exile in 1949, Mir helped to found the Popular Socialist Party, later to become the Dominican Communist Party. Following his return to the country in the 1960s, Mir widened his output to include historical texts, short stories and novels, maintaining a radical focus on historical and contemporary social change. *Cuando amaban las tierras comuneras* (When Communal Lands Were Loved), first published in 1978, charts the intimate relationship between the Dominican peasantry and their territorial patrimony, until foreign, namely U.S., intervention usurped the primordial balance between land and people. Mir's defiant nationalism, romanticism and literary dynamism have withstood, and indeed have grown through, the surrounding turmoil of his country's political and economic troubles.

A tradition of successfully combined literary and political interests is clearly exemplified by the former presidents, Joaquín Balaguer and Juan Bosch. Balaguer has produced several volumes of sensitive and reflective poetry, in stark contrast to his often ruthless methods of governance. Bosch, a respected academic, has gained international respect for his short story writing. *Cuentos escritos en el exilio* (1971) and *Más cuentos escritos en el exilio* (1975) illustrate an accomplished skill for incisive and evocatively descriptive prose.

Modern Dominican writers are increasingly making their mark on the international literary circuit. Junot Díaz and Julia Alvarez, among others, have established their reputations while living in the U.S., often using the experience of migration and cultural interaction as the thematic basis for their writing. Paradoxically, these writers have found success first in the U.S. before exporting their work back to their homeland. The Dominican Republic has a relatively high literacy rate of around 77 percent for both men and women, but only a minority of Dominicans spend their spare time with their heads in a book. Besides music and dancing, any visitor to the country soon recognizes the consummate national passion for baseball which involves the majority of the population.

Baseball

Commentators have observed, only half in amusement, that there has never been a revolution during the baseball season in the Dominican Republic. Baseball reigns as the national sport, but it originated as an American import. Some would argue that the game deliberately followed the North American flag during the final decade of the nineteenth century as cultural imperialism shadowed economic and political imperatives.

Amateur baseball thrived in the Dominican Republic from the beginning of the twentieth century, having been brought across from Cuba. The flourishing professionalism of the game gave rise to an intense rivalry between two teams, Licey and Escogido, the blues and the reds respectively. The combatants' colors were reminiscent of the two mainstream political parties; baseball thus became emblematic of wider societal and political struggles.

Baseball on the streets of Santo Domingo   *AP Photo/John Riley*

The U.S. occupation between 1916 and 1924 undoubtedly served to strengthen the grip of baseball as the national sport. Dominican players began to be drawn overseas to professional leagues in Puerto Rico, Cuba, Venezuela and, most notably, the U.S. Escalating salaries at home and abroad gave baseball stars added economic and cultural status. Neither was their political impact insignificant. Fellito Guerra, a Dominican baseball legend during the 1920s, was asked to play in the U.S. leagues, the ultimate promotion for island players. His refusal expressed popular rejection of the U.S. occupation at the time.

The 1937 baseball season in the Dominican Republic marked the zenith of the national game, before U.S. capital and teams became dominant. The three leading teams — Santiago, Estrellas Orientales from San Pedro de Macorís, and the newly formed Ciudad Trujillo — battled out a passionate 36-game series, during which wild spending and costly imported players exhausted the sport's finances. Whereas today's game is characterized by the flow of players to the North American mainland, the 1930s saw the increasing import of African Americans from the Negro Leagues of the U.S. Ciudad Trujillo, in particular, a team created and funded for the single season by Trujillo to cater to his baseball-mad brother, was foremost in luring overseas players with extravagant salaries. The professional sport blew itself out, but by the early 1950s it had recovered sufficiently to witness the short-lived golden age of Dominican baseball, the so-called beísbol romantico, during which local rather than foreign interests underpinned the game. The passion of fans, players and owners were immersed in what was not only a truly national game, but arguably boasted the best exponents in the world.

After 1955, the U.S. major leagues clearly dominated Dominican baseball. Teams such as the Dodgers and Yankees established "working relationships" with Dominican counterparts. The trickle of Dominican players who went to the U.S. in the 1950s had gushed to hundreds by the 1980s. Free agency agreements and the rise of U.S.-owned feeder academies in the Dominican Republic restructured the dominance of American interests. As minimum salaries soared from an already substantial $12,000 in the 1970s to over $125,000 today, the major leagues have become increasingly bright beacons of escape for aspiring Dominican baseball stars.

Alex Rodríguez is the latest young star to seize the Dominican sporting imagination. A batting average of .358 may mean little to the uninformed; 215 hits and 36 home runs may again fail to raise the eyebrows of the uninitiated, but an annual income of $2.5 million will normally provoke comment from even the most committed baseball-phobe. To Dominican *fanáticos* all the figures spell magic and sum up the lure of major league baseball. Rodríguez is the 21-year-old new Dominican kid on the ballpark. Voted the Dominican Baseball Player of the Year in 1996, he plays for the Seattle Mariners, and now joins the hallowed ranks of players such as Sammy Sosa, José Rijo, Ramón Martínez and Mélido Pérez who have all made the big time. These figures are not only sporting icons, heroes of super-salaried success, but underline the power and enchantment which baseball possesses in Dominican society.

While most Dominicans will never have the opportunity to see their top Major League stars other than on the TV screen, the national league provides more than enough live action. Between October and February each year, the Dominican baseball season opens up to receive its fanatical supporters. Merely the approach to a stadium in Santo Domingo, Santiago or San Pedro de Macóris on the night of a big game becomes a mass spectacle in itself. Agitated scalpers flash tickets at the crowds lined up. Car watchers usher those with vehicles to the safety of their personally guarded parking lots. Once inside the stadium, the noise, excitement and incessant buzz reach a crescendo well before the first ball has been pitched, although concurring with Dominican norms, a proportion of the crowd arrives late, filtering in at some stage during the early innings. Failing loudspeakers feebly attempt to echo announcements above the commotion. If not drowned out by the noise of the crowd, their attempts will be lost to the tinny melodies of an ad hoc *merengue* assemble. Throughout the game, *tigueritos* and hawkers aim to earn a day's living, taking bets or selling food and drinks. The stadium bubbles as a hive of activity on and off the ballpark, a ritualized weekly necessity for players, patrons and fans.

WHERE TO GO, WHAT TO SEE

A new domestic flight schedule introduced in 1997 means that visitors can cover a range of locations and cities with relatively ease, although the two national coach companies continue to provide good and efficient, if less rapid, services. A host of smaller, private companies provides regular and reliable inter-town travel. If you are staying at a beach resort, the effort made to get outside the perimeter of the complex will be well rewarded. You may be warned of the dangers lurking beyond the tourist trail, but common sense is the surest safeguard against mishap. A basic knowledge of Spanish will be helpful, but the lack of it is not an insurmountable hindrance. The main restriction on independent travel beyond the tourist locations tends to be that of uninformed fear. A little knowledge of Spanish makes local newspapers an interesting purchase: the type of story which gains the headlines can tell the visitor as much about the country as the news itself.

Starting in the capital, Santo Domingo, history enthusiasts will want to head straight for the former colonial zone. The city's old quarter on the west bank of the Ozama River houses the architectural splendors which date from the first 50 years after Columbus's arrival. The first cathedral, fort, governor's residence and central plaza of the emerging Spanish empire are all to be found, many of the buildings sensitively restored. El Conde, the pedestrian spine which leads out from the shady plaza overlooked by the statue of Columbus, is lined with superstores, cafes and restaurants. Empty under the midday sun, the mall bustles into life during mid-afternoons, virtually erupting at the weekends. Regular street markets and exhibitions outshine the inherent dullness of a 1970s-inspired consumer's walkway. Step off the mall and you are drawn down the quieter, architecturally eclectic streets of downtown Santo Domingo. A few corner stores, bookstores and restaurants, nestled between colonial churches and nineteenth-century town houses, make an hour's wander a highly-recommended detour.

Stretching farther west from the center, the visitor comes across Gazcue, formerly the haunt of Trujillo's favored followers. Much of the formerly fashionable housing from the 1930s and 1940s hovers on the edge of disrepair. Nevertheless, the mellow tree-lined streets retain a strongly middle-class population, and several new apartment blocks have developed an air of modernity. The Gazcue neighborhood retains some of its distinction by containing the presidential palace and the 1970s, Balaguer-built *Plaza de la Cultura,* home of the National Theater, Library, Art Gallery and Museums.

To the east of the city center, a bus, *carro* or taxi-ride away lies Columbus's lighthouse, *El Faro a Colón*, which has become an attraction more through the controversy surrounding its construction than architectural merit or historical record. At night on the weekends, this quincentennial folly casts out a cross-shaped beam of light above the suburbs of Santo Domingo. Great for tourists and some townsfolk, less so for those restricted to candlelight on Friday and Saturday night as the electricity supply falters.

Moving out of the capital, 15 miles to the east along palm-lined seaside roads are the reef-protected and shallow waters of Boca Chica beach resort, one of the most popular beaches in the south of the island, not least because it lies within easy reach of the waves of weekend metropolitan sun-seekers. Further east, traveling along the Mella highway which skirts a series of good beaches, are the towns of San Pedro de Macorís and La Romana. They are interesting sugar towns for a day's visit, and very much characteristic of small-town Dominican society. Leaving La Romana, the road passes the Casa de Campo resort and heads for Higüey, the location of the *Basilica de Nuestra Señora de la Altagracia*, and the pilgrimage site for thousands of Dominicans who come to pray before the country's patron saint. Every year on January 21, the devout visit the sacred shrine at the heart of the strikingly designed, modern cathedral which dominates the surrounding cane fields.

To the west of Santo Domingo, the highway passes through the industrial port of Haina and the small town of San Cristóbal, the birthplace of the dictator Trujillo. Beyond, the town of Barahona and the southwest coast have been perennially short-listed for tourist development. Little concrete growth can be seen, but those with transportation can view the spectacular coastlines of white sand beaches and plunging, wooded cliffs. To the north, the lush region around Azua and San Juan de la Maguana lies in stark contrast to the barren approach to the Haitian border. A trip to Lago Enriquillo is a recommended excursion, offering an expansive inland sea, surrounded by impenetrable scrub, yet providing sustenance for an impressive range of flora and fauna. Onwards to the border, the traveler encounters dusty frontier towns such as Elías Piña, Jimaní and Dajabón to the north, and an ever-growing number of military checkpoints, staffed by despondent-looking soldiers with ancient weaponry and nothing much to do.

Traveling north from Santo Domingo, along the newly widened Duarte Highway, the visitor realizes why all the other regional roads are relatively quiet. The main drag between the capital and the second city of Santiago de los Caballeros, seems always to be busy. Cars, buses and trucks drive along at breakneck speed, hurtling through impressive scenery. The central highlands lie to the west, lush farmland and plantations to the east. The towns of Constanza and Jarabacoa are good destinations if you wish to escape the lowland heat and to organize a trek through the hills. Santiago

Puerto Plata central plaza

David Howard

itself is an interesting place in which to spend a day or so. Enjoy the locally produced coffee in the cafes, visit the tobacco and rum factories and climb up the steps of the imposing Monument to the War of Restoration, a tower perched on the city's highest point, overlooking the suburbs and to the Cibao valley beyond. During the evenings, hundreds of santiagueros, young and old, gather here to hang out above the busy downtown streets below.

Further north on the Amber Coast lies the attractive town of Puerto Plata, with tourist resorts stretching to the east. The central square is still a good place to while away time, and the fort, a short walk along the Malecón, is an interesting break from the beach. Traveling east along the coast, the highway passes through the resort of Sosúa and the quieter beachside towns of Río San Juan and Nagua, arriving at Sánchez — a small town on the beautiful Samaná Bay. From here you can reach the exquisite, and not overly developed, beaches of Las Terrenas and Las Galeras, or take a boat trip to the mangrove swamps and caves located around the bay. Further east lies Samaná, the starting point for whale watching and boats trip to the Cayo Levantado, the Bacardi-commercial isle.

If you have the chance to travel beyond the major cities or resorts, then do so. You'll appreciate a little more of the finer things Dominican, from a few moments spent mulling over life events while seated on the plaza or in a corner *colmado* away from the crowds.

TIPS FOR TRAVELERS

Climate and Clothing

The Dominican Republic has a warm-to-hot climate all year-round, with frequent rainy afternoons from May to September. Temperatures range from a pleasant heat in the winter months, to what can be a sweltering and fatigue-inducing humidity during the midsummer. Temperatures hover around the eighties, although combine the humidity with a ten-minute ride in a *carro*, and you will gain the nearest experience to a sauna on wheels. The visitor should bring a range of light clothes, although bear in mind that in Santo Domingo the dress code can range from laid-back to absurdly formal, depending on the venue. The National Theater aims to maintain its high-culture status by briskly warning theater-goers that they must wear socks and be of smart appearance, with strictly no jeans or casual sports shoes allowed. Few of the audience seem ever to be barred or ejected for shoddy appearance, but you have been warned. In general, a night on the town requires a certain level of aesthetic preparation in the clothes department, or at least the recognition that Dominicans, in general, do dress to impress and are unlikely to rate the casual jet-set or traveler's grunge look. Winter may require a light sweater to be packed in the suitcase, useful for wrapping purchases on the way back if nothing else, but warm waterproof clothing should undoubtedly be brought along if you intend to go walking in the central mountains whatever the season. Catching hypothermia in the Caribbean may sound a good story to recount in retrospect, but as the mountain rain descends and temperatures drop, the hilarity of the situation also rapidly plummets. The author writes from miserable experience.

Money

All fitted out and ready to set forth on a daytime shopping quest or night-time rum and *merengue* bonanza, the visitor will need some currency. Within a few strides along El Conde, you'll be offered the chance to exchange money. Don't. Too many tourists have lost too many dollars for it to be worth the novelty of discovering an honest money exchanger in Santo Domingo. You may indeed achieve a satisfactory cash deal, but you will also probably unwittingly have lost a watch, bag or camera during the pleasantries of the transaction. The airport *casas de cambio* generally have good rates if you need cash on arrival, and all major banks will offer a standard exchange service, often within the welcome luxury of an air-conditioned office. That sweater may yet be of use if the air-conditioning is particularly efficient. Fourteen Dominican pesos are (as of 1998) the equivalent to one U.S. dollar. Pound sterling travelers' checks may be cashed in banks or large hotels, but you would be strongly advised to bring only U.S. dollar travelers' checks. All medium-to-large hotels, restaurants and commercial establishments will gladly accept the major credit cards.

Security

Although Dominican newspapers complain that life is getting more dangerous on the streets of Santo Domingo (allegedly due to the increasing numbers of ne'er-do-well Dominicans being deported from New York's prisons), the visitor has little to fear if she or he adopts a common sense approach. As a tourist, you may be particularly attractive to petty criminals, but sensible precautions such as not flashing wads of *pesos* in public view, being aware of your surroundings if it's late or particularly busy, and keeping an eye on your possessions (much as you would do back home) will generally keep you away from trouble. Petty theft in beach resorts is rare but not unknown, so you would be wise to watch out for your belongings, especially if you wander away from popular locations.

Women Travelers

The overly expressive *machismo* of Dominican men will mean that most women visitors will at some time be hailed as the "most beautiful rose to flower under Caribbean skies," "the most gorgeous women to grace the streets of Santo Domingo," or other expressions of that ilk. While incessant streams of verbal "appreciation" can be trying, annoying and a drain on everyday sanity, male attention should be expected. Very rarely do the approaches develop beyond banter, but Dominican men (accepting the often gross injustice of stereotypes) tend to be insistent in their advances unless overt lack of interest is expressed. It is as well to remember that this attentive approach is the norm in Dominican society, not just an exasperating trait saved solely for foreign women.

Children and Health

Children can be happily accommodated on a trip to the Dominican Republic. All that a baby requires can be found in the supermarket or pharmacy (usually U.S. brands), although the tap water should be avoided by infants and adults alike. There is a wide range of bottled water available, and most Dominicans do not drink unbottled water unless they are forced. Unfortunately, given the poor quality of water provision, this means that many do have to use contaminated water sources. Food from cheap restaurants and street sellers can cause stomach upsets.

Most visitors to the country do not require a visa, but will need to purchase a tourist card for $10 on arrival at the airport. The period of stay is initially 60 days, but visits can be extended. You will have to pay a small fine of $2 (which may or may not reach government coffers) at the airport on departure for each month of extra stay.

ADDRESSES AND CONTACTS

AmeriSpan Unlimited
PO Box 40007
Philadelphia, PA 19106-0007
http://www.amerispan.com
(volunteers and interns)

Journey Latin America
14-16 Devonshire Road
London W4 2BR
Tel: (0181) 747-3108

Embassy of the Dominican Republic
1715 22nd Street, NW
Washington D.C. 20008
Tel: (202) 332-6280

Consulate of the Dominican Republic
15 Brechin Place
London SW7 4QB

National Parks Office
Avenida Independencia 539
Santo Domingo

FURTHER READING AND BOOKSTORES

Balaguer, J. *La isla al revés: Haití y el destino dominicano*. Santo Domingo, 1993.
Bell, I. *The Dominican Republic*. Boulder, CO, 1981.
Black, J. K. *The Dominican Republic: Politics and Development in an Unsovereign State*. London, 1986.
Bosch, J. *The Unfinished Experiment: Democracy in the Dominican Republic*. London, 1965.
Calder, B. J. *The Impact of Intervention: the Dominican Republic During the U.S. Occupation of 1916-1924*. Austin, TX, 1984.
Crassweller, R. D. *Trujillo: The Life and Times of a Caribbean Dictator*. New York, 1964.
Ferguson, J. *The Dominican Republic: Beyond the Lighthouse*. London/ New York, 1992.
Galíndez, J. de. *The Era of Trujillo: Dominican Dictator*. Tucson, 1974.
Georges, E. *The Making of a Transnational Community: Migration, Development and Cultural Change in the Dominican Republic*. New York, 1990.
Grasmuck, S. and Pessar, P. R. *Between Two Islands: Dominican International Migration*. Berkeley, CA, 1991.
Hendricks, G. *Dominican Diaspora: From the Dominican Republic to New York City — Villagers in Transition*. New York, 1974.
Hoetink, H. *The Dominican People, 1850-1900*. Baltimore, 1982.
Lemoine, M. *Bitter Sugar*. London, 1985.
Moya Pons, F. *Manual de historia dominicana* (ninth edition). Santo Domingo, 1992.
Plant, R. Sugar and Modern Slavery: *a Tale of Two Countries*. London, 1986.
Vega, B. et al. *Ensayos sobre la cultura dominicana*. Santo Domingo, 1988.
Wiarda, H. J. and M. J. Kryzanek. *The Dominican Republic: a Caribbean Crucible*. Boulder, CO, 1992.

Fiction

Alvarez, J. *How the Garcia Girls Lost Their Accent*. New York, 1991.
Alvarez, J. *In the Time of the Butterflies*. New York, 1994.
Díaz, J. *Drown*. New York/London, 1996.
Galván, M. de J. *Enriquillo* (1889) *(The Cross and the Sword.)* London, 1956.
Hernández Franco, T. *Yelidá* (1942). Santo Domingo, 1985.

Marrero Aristy, R. *Over* (1940). Santo Domingo, 1992.
Prestol Castillo, F. *El masacre se pasa a pie.* Santo Domingo, 1973.

Local Bookstores

Tienda Macalé
Calle Arzobispo Nouel 3
Santo Domingo

The Book Shop
Plaza Cataluña/Gustavo Mejía Ricart 114
Santo Domingo

La Trinitaria
Calle Arzobispo Nouel 158
Santo Domingo

Cuesta: Centro del Libro
Avenida 27 de Febrero/Abraham Lincoln
Santo Domingo

FACTS AND FIGURES

GEOGRAPHY

Official name: La República Dominicana.

Situation: between 17° and 19° N, and 68° and 72° W, the eastern two-thirds of the island of Hispaniola, bordering Haiti. The Dominican Republic is the second largest, by land area and population size, of the Caribbean island states.

Surface area: 18,811 square miles (48,734 square kilometers).

Climate: tropical maritime climate with average temperatures ranging from 78°F (January) to 86°F (July); the rainy season lasts from May to November, contributing to an annual rainfall of 60 inches.

Relief: the highest mountain in the Caribbean, Pico Duarte (10,500 feet above sea level), is located in the central mountain range of the Cordillera Central which crosses the country from northwest to southeast. Lowland coastal areas and the fertile Cibao valley are the main regions of agricultural production and population settlement. The southern coastal plains have historically been the focus of sugar-cane production, while tobacco and cocoa production is concentrated in the cooler valleys and agricultural areas to the north, especially the Cibao. Sandy beaches are to be found all around the coast, although the shoreline be-

tween Santo Domingo and La Romana is characterized by more rocky outcrops.

Flora and fauna: The Dominican Republic contains a varied range of natural habitats, from the upland pine forests of the Cordillera Central, to the desert scrub of the border zone, to the vast plains of fertile coastal soils. The inland sea of Lago Enriquillo provides a unique environment for cacti, scrubland vegetation, and an interesting array of fauna such as crocodiles, iguanas and 45 native bird species. The latter include manuelitos, hummingbirds, querebebes and cu-cus. The green cotica parrot is the national bird — often kept as a pet. Many coastal regions provide a rich variety of vegetation, such as the mangroves in the Los Haitises National Park near Samaná, and the dry sub-tropical forest near Montecristi, both on the northern coast. National parks, areas for scientific research, and other protected zones have been established by the government to conserve lagoons, river estuaries, islands, bays, upland forest, and marine eco-systems. Samaná has gained an international reputation as a point of departure for whale-watching trips to the surrounding breeding grounds of Banco de la Plata

(Silver Banks). Endangered species include the manatee and the *hutia*, an indigenous rodent. The Dominican Republic is currently the location for a United Nations-backed Global Biodiversity program.

Administrative divisions: 29 Provinces and 1 National District.

Capital: Santo Domingo, 2.2 million (1995).

Other principal cities: Santiago 467,000; La Vega 189,000; San Francisco de Macorís 162,000; San Pedro de Macorís 137,000 (1995).

Infrastructure: there are 2,700 miles of roads linking all the main towns and resorts areas, most are paved. The busiest and best-maintained route is the Duarte Highway, which links the capital, Santo Domingo, with the second city, Santiago de los Caballeros, and the coastal town of Puerto Plata to the north. There are no passenger rail services, although 990 miles of track exist to serve the sugar industry. The country is well-served by air as a tourist destination with five international airports. The national airline, Dominicana Airlines, however, ceased operations in 1995. An improved domestic air service was established in 1996, serving a range of destinations across the country.

DOMINICAN REPUBLIC
National Parks

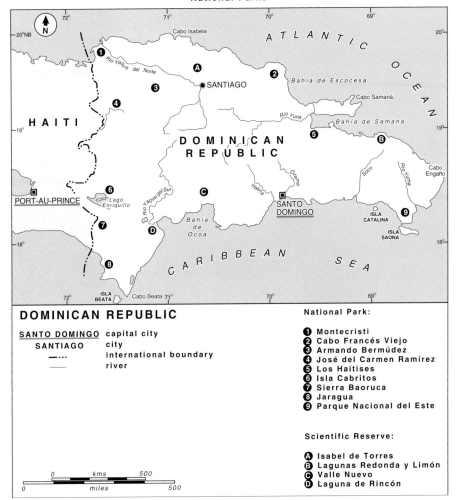

DOMINICAN REPUBLIC

SANTO DOMINGO   capital city
SANTIAGO   city
—...—   international boundary
——   river

0   kms   500
0   miles   500

National Park:

1 Montecristi
2 Cabo Francés Viejo
3 Armando Bermúdez
4 José del Carmen Ramírez
5 Los Haitises
6 Isla Cabritos
7 Sierra Baoruca
8 Jaragua
9 Parque Nacional del Este

Scientific Reserve:

A Isabel de Torres
B Lagunas Redonda y Limón
C Valle Nuevo
D Laguna de Rincón

DOMINICAN REPUBLIC
Climate and Vegetation Zones

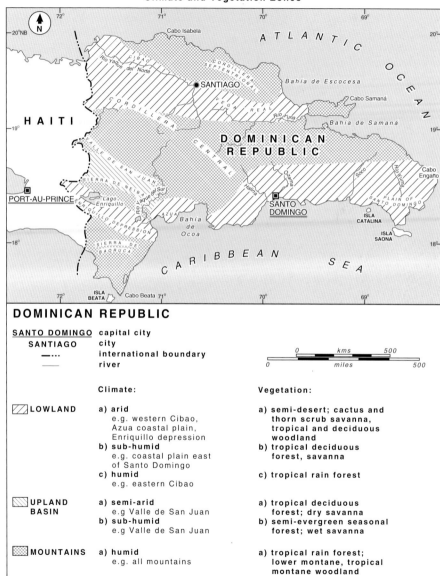

DOMINICAN REPUBLIC

SANTO DOMINGO	capital city
SANTIAGO	city
—·...	international boundary
——	river

0   kms   500
0   miles   500

Climate:

LOWLAND
a) arid
e.g. western Cibao, Azua coastal plain, Enriquillo depression
b) sub-humid
e.g. coastal plain east of Santo Domingo
c) humid
e.g. eastern Cibao

UPLAND BASIN
a) semi-arid
e.g Valle de San Juan
b) sub-humid
e.g Valle de San Juan

MOUNTAINS
a) humid
e.g. all mountains

Vegetation:

a) semi-desert; cactus and thorn scrub savanna, tropical and deciduous woodland
b) tropical deciduous forest, savanna
c) tropical rain forest

a) tropical deciduous forest; dry savanna
b) semi-evergreen seasonal forest; wet savanna

a) tropical rain forest; lower montane, tropical montane woodland

POPULATION

Population: 7,823,000 (1995). *Population growth rate:* 3.6 % (1960s); 2.4% (1981-93); 1.2% (1992-2000). *Urban population:* 63 % (1995). *Rural population:* 37 % (1995). *Population density:* 162 per square km (1995). *Languages:* Spanish; about 300,000 speak Haitian Kreyòl (Creole). *Ethnic composition:* most Dominicans are of Spanish and African descent. *Population by age:* 0-14 years 37.9 %; 15-64 years 58.7 %; over 65 years 3.4 %. *Children per woman:* 3 (1992). *Life expectancy:* female 64.0 years; male 60.0 years (1995). *Infant mortality rate:* 21 per 1000 live births (1995). *Health provision:* One physician for every 935 inhabitants (1991).

Average calorie consumption: 95% of recommended intake (1995). *Extended family average per household:* 14 members (1995). *Access to electricity:* 38 % (1993). *Direct access to potable water:* 76 % (1995). *Communications:* 8 national daily newspapers; 100 TV sets and 93 radio sets per 1000 households; 7.4 telephones per 100 inhabitants (1995). *Literacy rates:* 77% for men and women (1996). *Education:* 99% female and male children are enrolled for primary school; 43% female and 30% male children are enrolled for secondary school (1995). Primary education (8 years, starting at the age of 7) is free and compulsory. In

1989, there was one primary school teacher for every 47 pupils. Secondary education is wholly maintained by the state or is state-aided and includes normal, vocational and special schools. In 1998 there were 4 universities, 3 Roman Catholic universities, 1 Adventist university, 3 technological universities and 5 other tertiary education institutes. In 1994, 18% of adults attended tertiary education. *Religion:* The official state religion is Roman Catholicism, with 91% of the population defining themselves as Catholic in 1997. *Social development index:* (UNDP Human Development Index 1996): 87th position out of total 174 positions (U.S. 3rd position, UK 16th, Haiti 145th).

HISTORY AND POLITICS

Some key dates: *?-1000 AD: the island of Quisqueya discovered and settled by Amerindian groups migrating from mainland America * 1492: Columbus lands on the island (renamed Hispaniola) * 1496: the brother of Columbus, Bartolomé, founds the city of Santo Domingo, the oldest European-established city in the Americas * 1520s: following the extermination of indigenous groups through illness, enslavement and repres-

sion, the large scale importation of slaves from West Africa begins * 1562: an earthquake devastates many Spanish settlements in the north of the country * 1560s increasing harassment of coastal settlements by French and British buccaneers * 1586: Francis Drake sacks Santo Domingo * 1697: the western part of the languishing Spanish colony of Hispaniola is ceded to France under the Treaty of Ryswick * 1740: the

population of the Spanish colony on the eastern two-thirds of the island numbers only 6,000 * 1795: France gains nominal control of the whole island under the Treaty of Basle * 1801-1803: the Haitian leader, Toussaint L'Ouverture, occupies Santo Domingo * 1804: Haitian independence declared * 1822-1844: after ongoing hostilities, Haitian forces govern the whole island * 1844: declaration of Dominican independence following the defeat of occupying Haitian forces * 1861: the re-establishment of Spanish sovereignty at the request of the Dominican President Pedro Santana * 1865: second declaration of independence and establishment of the Dominican Republic following the defeat of Spanish forces during the War of Restoration * 1882-1899: the dictatorship of Ulises Heureaux stands out as a notable exception from five confused decades of short-lived governments and economic instability since independence was restored * 1905: the inability of the country to pay external creditors leads to the establishment of customs receivership by the U.S. * 1916-1924: U.S. occupation of the Dominican Republic * 1930: Rafael Leónidas Trujillo Molina, commanding general of the new U.S.-trained national guard is elected President and establishes a 32-year dictatorship, which includes the nominal puppet presidencies of Trujillo's brother, Héctor (1947-60), and Dr Joaquín Balaguer (1960-1962) * 1961: assassination of the dictator Trujillo * 1962: Juan Bosch, leader of the Dominican Revolutionary Party (PRD) is elected as President, takes office in February 1963, but is overthrown by a military coup after only seven months * 1963: a three-man civilian junta, La

Trinitaria, is established * 1965: opponents of La Trinitaria and its military backers launch an insurrection on 24 April; four days later a force of 23,000 U.S. marines land on the island and a peace force under the aegis of the Organization of American States is subsequently established * 1966-1978: Balaguer, leader of the Christian Social Reform Party (PRSC), is elected President following the April Revolution and maintains power during a decade of urban terrorism, military coup attempts and corruption * 1978-1986: the PRD elected for two terms, marked by the suicide in office of President Silvestre Antonio Guzmán and by increasing economic turmoil and popular protests * 1986-1996: Balaguer regains power, dominating the political scene for the ensuing decade, assisted by divisions in the opposition PRD and widely recognized claims of fraudulent electoral practices * 1996: with Balaguer unable to stand for re-election, Dr Leonel Fernández is elected President as leader of the Dominican Liberation Party following a second-round electoral pact with the PRSC * 1997: a turbulent year of public protest and strikes.

Constitution: a representative democracy, with legislative power resting in a bicameral congress — a 30-seat Senate and a 120-seat Chamber of Deputies. Senators and deputies are elected on a four-yearly basis, as is the president.

Head of State: Dr Leonel Fernández (elected August 1996). He gained 51.25% of votes cast in the deciding second round of the presidential elections.

Main political parties (with seats in Chamber of Deputies and Senate after 1996 elections): PRD — Partido Revolucionario Dominicano (Dominican Revolutionary Party) 57 (15); PRSC — Partido Reformista Social Cristiano (Christian Social Reform Party) 50 (14); PLD — Partido de la Liberación Dominicana (Dominican Liberation Party) 13 (1). An alliance between the PRSC and PLD ensured victory for the PLD leader, Leonel Fernández.

Social organization: Most formal-sector workers are represented by the General Workers' Union (CGT) and the Unity Workers' Union (CUT).

Military personnel: 24,500 (army 15,000; navy 4,000; air force 5,500).

Military expenditure: 1.3% of GDP (1995).

Membership of international organizations: United Nations and UN organizations; Organization of American States; Association of Caribbean States.

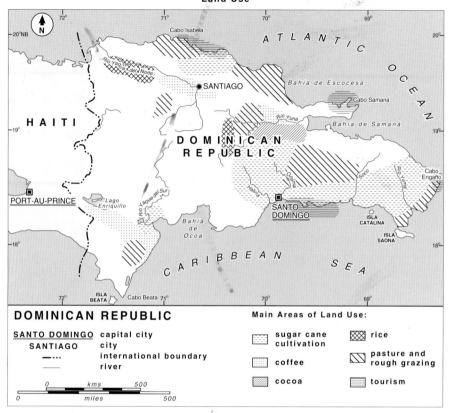

DOMINICAN REPUBLIC
Land Use

DOMINICAN REPUBLIC

SANTO DOMINGO capital city
SANTIAGO city
—...— international boundary
—— river

Main Areas of Land Use:

- sugar cane cultivation
- coffee
- cocoa
- rice
- pasture and rough grazing
- tourism

ECONOMY

Currency: peso (RD$); US$1= RD$14.26 (1997).
Inflation rate: 3.9% (1996); 8.4% (1997).
Gross Domestic Product (GDP): $13,200 million (1996).
Per capita GDP: $1,635 (1996).
Annual GDP growth rate: 4% (1994); 2.5% (1995); 7.3% (1996); 7.7% (1997).

GDP by sector (1996): Manufacturing 17 %; Agriculture, fishing and mining 12.9 %; Commerce 12.3%; Construction 10%; Government services 8.3%; Transport 6.8 %; others 22.7%.
Unemployment: 30 % (1990s).
Exports: $960 million (1996).
Imports: $3,650 million (1996).
Trade balance: — $2,690 million (1996).
Tourism earnings: $1,860 million (1997).
Free zone exports: $1,870 million (1996).
Remittance earnings (approximate): $800 million (1990s).
Principal exports (1996): ferro-nickel ($271m); sugar ($169.4m); tobacco ($100m); cocoa ($65m); coffee ($65m).